AFIRE *with* GOD

AFIRE
with
GOD

BECOMING SPIRITED STEWARDS

BETSY SCHWARZENTRAUB
with PAUL EXTRUM-FERNANDEZ,
MARIELLEN SAWADA,
AND ROBERT WILLIAMS

DISCIPLESHIP RESOURCES

PO BOX 340003 • NASHVILLE, TN 37203-0003
www.discipleshipresources.org

Cover design: Thelma Whitworth
Interior design & implementation: Nancy Cole-Hatcher
ISBN: 978-0-88177-520-4

AFIRE WITH GOD: Becoming Spirited Stewards

Library of Congress Cataloging-in-Publication Data on file.

For information regarding rights and permissions, contact Discipleship Resources, P.O. Box 340003, Nashville, TN 37203-0003; fax 615-340-1789.

CONTENTS

CHAPTER THREE

CHAPTER FOUR

PREFACE

This book is filled with the faces of people I have met through the years, people in congregations seeking a deeper sense of stewardship of the gospel. The writing process has been a community effort from the beginning, as I have learned from those who helped shape the book.

I am grateful to the Reverend Mariellen Sawada, Paul Extrum-Fernandez, and Robert Williams, my review team, who gave insights and practical examples from a variety of local churches. Their openness to seeing stewardship in a new light and discussing what works in different settings made this a lively team process.

Likewise, I learned much from Drs. Paul and Inagrace Dietterich of the Center for Parish Development. Through their four years of comprehensive stewardship training, they provided a foundational theology of the Holy Spirit and the Trinity and a system for how congregations can work and move toward positive change.

The writings of Henry H. Knight, III, were invaluable in understanding John Wesley's means of grace. Bradley Call's research provided essential information for generational stewardship. Melvin West, editor of the United Methodist Rural Fellowship Bulletin, contributed greatly to my information about the stewardship of the earth. I also appreciate the contributions of the Reverends Timothy Bagwell, Wayne Barrett, Brian Bauknight, Donald joiner, Herbert Mather, Douglas Meeks, Thomas Rieke, and Mark Vincent and the leaders of the 1999 North American Stewardship Conference for their illuminating writing and workshops.

This book is dedicated to Ken,
my soul mate for a lifetime and beyond.

—BETSY SCHWARZENTRAUB

INTRODUCTION

... Earth's crammed with heaven,
And every common bush afire with God:
But only he who sees, takes off his shoes,
The rest sit round it and pluck blackberries ...[1]

Stewardship is a dirty word in most self-respecting main-line churches these days. Periodically pastors may preach on stewardship with a mixture of biblical clarity and personal embarrassment in their eyes. For many church members, merely mentioning the word conjures up images of the annual struggle to "meet the budget" and then strip program dreams down to bare essentials after a disappointing financial response. The term may remind some members of painfully generic "it's-that-time-again" letters or confirm childhood messages about not tithing and eternal damnation. The word may steel members for those frantic, frequently labor-intensive, less-than-effective fund-raisers or for hard-sell techniques of "your money or your life."

So why talk about stewardship? Well, what if stewardship means something far different from, something broader and deeper than, hair-raising techniques or frustrating approaches? What if lively, authentic stewardship holds the key to our spiritual journey as individuals and as congregations? What if stewardship is a way we can live out the gospel positively afire with God?

But watch out. Real stewardship is radical, which means going to the roots of our faith. If we take stewardship seriously—and joyfully—it won't be just another addition to the same old programs we've been doing in our congregations. It will change our thinking, acting, and imagining. It will alter our identity as a community of stewards of the gospel of Jesus Christ. And it will change our vision of ministry, working from the inside out.

Afire with God invites us to rethink our identity and ministry as the body of Christ as it relates to stewardship. Chapter one addresses the reasons many of us are both reluctant and ambivalent about discussing "the S word" in today's world. It examines what is not working in our old way of doing stewardship. Then it points to how we can move toward a vibrant, faithful stewardship of the gospel and of all that God has entrusted to us.

Chapter two uses Moses' experience at the burning bush as a metaphor to explore stewardship foundations in the Scripture. This chapter examines the stewardship thread that weaves through the Bible, explaining and deepening our sense of personal and corporate response to God.

Chapter three recalls our tradition as stewards of God's mysteries, beginning with God's commandments and the concept of repairing the world. Then the discussion moves to the Trinity and stewardship as participation in God at work. Finally, chapter three relates stewardship to John Wesley's means of grace and to Wesley's own life as a steward.

Chapter four looks at practical approaches for becoming stewards-in-action, with examples from various North American congregations. These approaches include reshaping the offering to become a highlight of worship; encouraging individual spiritual-growth stewardship opportunities; creating a climate for generous giving; responding to the variety of giving patterns within the congregation; preaching the richness of biblical stewardship; experiencing freedom in proportionate giving; practicing stewardship year round, from ministry-planning to evaluation; mobilizing people's time, talents, and individual spiritual gifts; focusing on the views and experiences of each generation; and funding the church for ministry.

So now to begin . . .

Endnotes

1. From *Aurora Leigh*, "Seventh Book," by Elizabeth Barrett Browning, 1864.

CHAPTER ONE

✠

Aliens in Egypt: Reluctant Stewards in a Complex World

Using the S Word

If evangelism is telling the good news of God's love, then stewardship is showing the good news by the way we live. Stewardship is both individual and corporate TLC—Total Life Commitment to God's purposes on earth, and Tender Loving Care for every dimension of life as a trust from God.

Stewardship is a continuous cycle that begins with God's initiative and gifts, and continues with our receiving, managing, and distributing all that God has entrusted to us. Stewardship involves investing our passions, abilities, and commitments in every dimension of living. Such a stewardship perspective sparks an intentional plan to grow year round as we dialogue constantly with the Scriptures, asking faith questions that push beyond religiosity and tug at the edges of our comfort zone.

Living as stewards brings tough questions to our lives. For example, do our time-planners, credit cards, and checkbooks reveal that we are good stewards in our families and congregations? How do we prioritize our time, our assets, and the multiple demands on our lives? And what does all this have to do with "Spirited" stewardship, anyway?

Getting Out of Egypt

It's an odd feeling. Some of us used to feel at home in the church. We remember when the church was an accepted anchor in society, when we could open the doors and people would simply come. Others of us have come more recently in response to our spiritual journeys. We sense that God is on the move, and we want to be part of God's action but are unsure about how the church can help.

Either way, Christians can feel like aliens living in a wilderness between security left behind and a new home somewhere beyond the horizon. Like the early Hebrews trying to get out of Egypt, we bring conflicting loyalties and memories along with us. Remembering Pharaoh, we distrust any faith community that claims to lead us into the future.

But there's more. Sometimes we want the best of the old life and the new life together, without paying any personal cost. Couldn't we return to the days of the church-on-the-main-square social acceptability and at the same time keep our new understandings? We may even yearn for the imagined fish, leeks, onions, and garlic in the stew pots back in those good old days (see Numbers 11:4-6). The more we recall those years of easy church starts and burgeoning Sunday schools, the more of a Golden Age those years become—and the less we remember any limitations, restrictions, or slavery that went with them.

A number of signs tell us we can't go back to the way we were. Today we live in a smaller world. Our lives interweave, not only with multiple multinational economic threads but also with our Internet "neighbors." Western culture has become ethnically colorful, challenging us to redefine what we assume about diversity, homogeneity, and community life. The gap between "have" and "have-not" countries is widening. Environmental issues are now as vital to life and death as are global weapons and war. In the interface between humanity and scientific advance, we face enormous ethical issues.

Within the church we deal increasingly with long-term issues of vision and purpose. In *Transforming Congregations for the Future*, Loren Mead says that today is a time of triumphalism for conservative churches in the way that the 1950s were for mainline congregations. The challenge for mainstream denominations today is that of building the church as an apostolate, a community of those whom Jesus sends out to proclaim the good news.[1] Such a change will require transformation of the church's inner life in at least two ways: by reflecting the *koinonia* (Communion community) of the early church network, and by developing a ministry where the story of God's people comes alive in the power of the Spirit.

So there is no going back to the good old days. We can forget Egypt's real or imagined leeks and onions. The only way forward lies through the wilderness. When we try to do stewardship in this new frame, it can get pretty confusing. We stand in the midst of unfinished pasts and incomplete futures, often using the same church language as before but referring to a different reality.

More times than we like to admit, well-meaning church leaders and members have used the term *stewardship* as a cover-up for messages we do not mean to give. For example, many annual pledge campaign leaders speak about giving *to* the budget of their local church instead of encouraging people to give to God *through* the church in pursuit of common, vital personal goals. Institutional fundraisers (or clergy imitating them) may use hard-sell fundraising techniques. These efforts are like old strip-mining approaches. They go straight for the riches, leaving behind emotional tailings and open wounds on the congregation's scarred landscape.

Or we may err on the other side by becoming self-conscious about money talk, neglecting to share biblical guidelines, and implying that whatever you want to give is fine. We may become so "seeker-oriented" that we view worshipers as customers and encourage an individualistic pay-for-services approach to Christian community.

These misuses of the term *stewardship* make us reluctant stewards. We don't know what good steward-ship really is, whether we want it, how to do it, or whether it has anything substantial to do with our faith and lives.

Remember, first God got the slaves out of Egypt; but then came the more difficult work of getting Egypt out of the slaves. So too with us. Enslaving attitudes and assumptions limit our vision, fruitfulness, sense of self-worth, and ability to enlist others in God's work. Getting rid of the Egypt within us is a lifetime process.

Facing the Gap

When it comes to faith issues, the old adage is true: You can't leap a chasm in two small jumps. In this case, the chasm is between the real stewardship that is presented through our Scriptures and tradition, and the current lackluster reality of biblically groundless, mediocre fundraising.

Our first task is to notice the crevasse between where God intends us to be and our current percep-tions of who we are (our identity) and what we do (our ministry). We know we cannot simply shift from where we are by sheer willpower. More fine-tuning does not reorient the system. Studies of the North American church by the Center for Parish Development show a qualitative difference in our congregations when we seek to move from tuning or adapting to reorienting.[2]

Tuning and adapting are both operational (rather than strategic) change processes. One is proactive; the other is reactive. By contrast, reorienting affects the entire organizational system. It pushes us to find a new way to perceive, think, act, and value. It is frame-bending. We learn how to see and respond differently to the world.

Real Christian stewardship requires reorienting the assumptions, images, expectations, and behaviors we have taken for granted in our culture. It does not break from our biblical heritage but bends our frame of reference. Such reorientation is called a paradigm shift. It is like a new set of eyes through which we see the world and a new set of hands and feet to act in it.

In liberation theology the word for this re-creating process is *praxis*. It describes the way we learn by acting first, then reflecting, then acting once again, so that our concepts change according to our experiences, not the other way around. Our behavior moves us into new ways of perception and action.

One biblical word for this shift is transformation. In 2 Corinthians 5:16-17, Paul says, "From now on, therefore, we regard no one from a human point of view; . . . everything has become new!"

Making such a change means shifting our focus from the fragmented, institutional-oriented sense of ministry and identity that we have held in the past. It is like looking through a camera lens as it moves from telephoto to wide-angle. No longer do we start with congregational "in-house" issues such as facilities, equipment, and programs. Instead, the lens of biblical stewardship turns our attention to what is distinctive about our community as stewards of the gospel. We begin not with people's needs but with our particular identity and ministry as God's distinctive people here and now.

Changing our lens makes us face the gap between our current stewardship reality and where we want to be biblically and pragmatically. Then this new view urges us to work together from what we see and know from Scripture and from our particular Christian tradition.

Troubled Waters

When it comes to stewardship in the church, we know that something is not working. At least seven situations indicate problems beneath the surface of even the most contented congregations:

1. *Some church members and many community residents see local churches as unresponsive to their changing needs, goals, and values.* This is due in part to the language and models we use based on different generational assumptions. For example, in congregational funding, many church leaders prefer written communications that talk about self-sacrifice, meeting the budget, and loyalty to the church—all concepts familiar to the GI Generation (born from 1910 to 1927) and

the Pioneer or Silent Generation (born from 1928 to 1945). But Baby Boomers (born from 1946 to 1963) and Postmodern (born from 1964 to 1981) respond better to verbal and interactive media and life fulfillment—better to hands-on ministries, Miracle Sundays, and short-term commitments—than to sacrifice. We still have much to learn about the Millennial Generation (born from 1982 to 1999), but hands-on, experiential ways of learning will certainly be effective for them as well.

2. *While problems facing our congregations are complex, most church leaders still look for one-dimensional solutions.* In *The Crisis in the Churches: Spiritual Malaise, Fiscal Woe,* author Robert Wuthnow says a fiscal storm is engulfing middle-class churches regardless of their theology, reflecting a full spiritual crisis.[3] Middle class people, from stay-at-home moms to professionals who put in sixteen-hour days, feel the pressures of being expected to do more than is possible for them to do. Then they feel guilty for what they have not done and are anxious about their futures. The predicament becomes more stressed when money is supposed to be a private matter, not discussed in church.

Christian faith has deep theological resources, says Wuthnow, but we haven't known how to share them. Often clergy are silent about members' economic pressures and are more at ease talking about the poor on the street. For most middle-class members, the prospect of job loss is more than just a financial issue. As a part of positive Christian stewardship, they need a framework that offers ways to understand the economy and their roles in it as stewards of their work, time, and money.

3. *Within any given congregation, members have varying understandings of what stewardship is, yet many congregational leaders insist on using one stewardship approach for all.*

Some constituents see environmental issues as a crucial dimension of Christian stewardship; others view environmental stewardship as a politically partisan issue. Some people are longtime tithers; others do not see the need for pledging. Some members have not thought about a will or about giving beyond their lifetime; others press for a local-church endowment fund. And corporate advocacy issues (stewardship of justice, of relationships, of economic distribution) seem unconnected with faith for all but a few.

As a result of one-fits-all stewardship approaches, segments of the congregation hear a hit-and-miss message of Christian stewardship. They lose the opportunity for an intentional, year-round learning approach to stewardship as a holistic way of Christian living.

4. *Churches cannot assume that families are training their children in positive patterns of church attendance, percentage giving, tithing, and a growing personal commitment,* although long-time church members often expect such understanding and commitment.

An increasing number of church attendees—and even pastors—are arriving from other denominations or from no church background at all. Sometimes even clergy lack the perspective, theology, or skills required

to lead congregations toward generous stewardship.
They don't know how to shape a congregational climate that encourages people to give generously of their
resources, investing their time, finances, abilities, and
passions as part of a full expression of their faith.

Since constituents often come to church without
an existing framework of Christian discipleship, congregations need to find ways to teach the disciplines of
consistent worship attendance, prayer for the church
and world, pledging money and time, and participation
in congregational life.

5. *Many local churches struggle for economic survival
in a world where downsizing affects mainline denominations
on every level.* In such a climate, many of us talk stewardship but practice institutional maintenance. For
example, outreach ministries that attract the
unchurched are the hardest to initiate and the least
controversial for jurisdictional bodies to leave
unfunded.

6. *Church members experience inherent conflict
between Christian values within the church and the empha-
sis on success, status, and acceptance in society.* Every day
commercials bombard North Americans from television, radio, the Internet, magazines, billboards, newspa-
pers, and designer-label clothing. Their messages
redefine people as consumers, whose wants naturally
become needs. A person's "worth" is weighed in money
and fame. And even those who wish to improve society
don't assume that the church is a primary channel for
social good.

In such a context, shaping missional communities is a complex process. It challenges the ways of thinking and organizing that worked when Christianity was an assumed part of the fabric of civic social life. But we no longer live in an age when the church is supported by the state. Being the church of Jesus Christ today requires rediscovering our identity and ministry.

7. *Our external world is changing. People are much more isolated, so those who are poor have fewer access points to their more comfortable neighbors.*

People with financial means are cocooning. They can shop and entertain themselves through the Internet and cable television. By switching a channel, they can even worship in the comfort of their homes. Studies show that when people do go out, more of them do so as lone rangers. Most no longer participate in voluntary associations. They watch movies on video or cable at home, and they bowl not in leagues but alone. Look around you as you drive to work. One commuter per car is so much the norm that in many places the expressway carpool lane is for only two or more people.

Many of these changes result in a greater sense of isolation in today's North American culture. From hospitals to schools to transportation, people with an economic safety net see less and less of people without financial assets. What are we saying and doing as stewards with this growing portion of our church and community? Stewardship involves more than just how to use discretionary income.

Systems Thinking

With so many issues facing the church, it might be easy to give up hope. But crisis offers opportunity as well as danger. When "business as usual" cannot meet an urgent demand, church leaders may listen more deeply and dare to move in a different direction.

Quest for Quality is an approach to organizational life begun by W. Edwards Deming. Ezra Earl Jones, formerly General Secretary of the General Board of Discipleship of The United Methodist Church, applied this approach to the church. Jones wrote *Quest for Quality in the Church: A New Paradigm* (Discipleship Resources, 1993) and introduced United Methodist annual conferences to the Quest process as a way to reorient their thinking and behavior. While *Quest for Quality in the Church* is no longer in print, *A New Kind of Church: A Systems Approach* (Discipleship Resources, 2006) challenges leaders to think deeply about congregational systems.

A New Kind of Church identifies two challenges that always face the church. The first is staying centered on Christ. The second challenge is imaging and structuring the body of Christ in the world so that it can be who it is every day. The church lives in real time in the places where human hurts and hopes are both frightening and life-giving. The authors, Dan Dick and Evelyn Burry, understand that everything about us as a church is related to every other thing around us. Their work points us to the lifelong path of improvement for individuals who make up the body of Christ.

A systems approach can help us come to terms with the impact of multiple groups and dynamics in church organizational life. But no set of questions or insights will reorient church leaders and members if we continue to think mechanistically.

Mechanistic thinking is what happens when we act as if our church were a machine consisting of separate, replaceable parts. If one Sunday school program fails, we plug in another one. If one pastor doesn't work, we find a replacement. If one community outreach plan doesn't work, we pick up another one and fit it in.

Such mechanistic thinking tends to focus on single causes for problems instead of multiple factors. It looks for problems within each part instead of reflecting on how the whole system works together. And it seeks solutions by further breaking down the components. Systems thinking, on the other hand, moves to larger and larger wholes and looks at mutual causes and interdependence.

In *Leadership and the New Science*, Margaret Wheatley says that Newton's scientific worldview lies underneath mechanistic thinking, whereas leaders in a newer scientific theory, quantum mechanics, and the science of chaos move us toward thinking holistically. A Newtonian view sees organizations as if they're machines—fixed and predictable. But a quantum approach expects no generic model to fit each situation. It looks at organizations as conscious, stable, but ever-changing systems. Set boundaries give way to ever-changing relationships. Workers are whole people who seek their own goals. What counts is the process, not the structure. Living systems constantly renew themselves in an inter-connected process.[4]

This systems description is true of churches, as well. A congregation is a living organism. Each local church consists of interlacing teams, part of a continually changing, interdependent system. Our ministry is based not on programs but on God's activity in the lives of people. We depend upon God's transformation, both in who we are becoming and in what we can do in the world. If we do not truly expect the presence and work of the Holy Spirit, any systems approach to the church can become just another layer of in-house lingo.

Spirited Stewardship

Historically we haven't talked much about the Holy Spirit in the mainline western church. In many of our congregations, prayer is an eighteen-second silence between verbal rituals in worship, or a brief formality before getting on to committee business.

But what if we took the Spirit seriously, as a real Presence, as the fullness of God's present activity and active presence with us? What if we listened for the Spirit's expression around and among us, in the needs as well as the resources of our personal lives and communities outside the church? What if we viewed church members, not as consumers to buy our services or as volunteers to staff our programs, but as ministers uniquely called and empowered to do what only they can do as part of Christ's body active on earth?

It is this kind of action that we call Spirited ministry! While some aspects of the worship, sharing, and witness of such Spirited ministry might be familiar to us, other dimensions look and feel very different from the way we've done church in the past. The concept of Spirited ministry changes our sense of who we are (our identity) and of what we are here to do (our ministry). The Spirit urges us to pray first and then plan, not plan first and then pray.

So how might such ministry relate to stewardship? Spirited stewardship is a living process of growth in our personal and corporate relationship with God. Spirited stewardship changes our activities from a boring repetition of frustrated efforts into a dynamic, fluid indicator of our changing spiritual journey. Spirited stewardship transforms each local church into a community of stewards who seek multiple ways to express God's grace in advocacy and action.

Spirited stewardship is whatever we do with the gospel through the way we live. It includes the ways we steward the good news, the ways we use our time and abilities, and the ways we identify and employ our spiritual gifts. It includes how we make and stick to our personal and family financial plans, what we choose to do with long-term assets to give beyond our lifetime, and how we deploy our ministry and even the congregation itself as a resource for all of God's people. And Spirited stewardship includes how we care for all of

God's creation. A congregation that practices Spirited
stewardship nurtures a high-quality relationship in
which members support common ministries, not just
the events that their groups plan.

First Peter 4:10-11 says:

> Like good stewards of the manifold grace of God, serve
> one another with whatever gift each of you has
> received. Whoever speaks must do so as one speaking
> the very words of God; whoever serves must do so with
> the strength that God supplies, so that God may be glo-
> rified in all things through Jesus Christ. To him belong
> the glory and the power forever and ever. Amen.

We know God's grace in many forms, through the
unique gifts not only of our individual members but also
of our quirky congregational personalities. As stewards
acting on behalf of God, we are called to be flexible and
responsive to human beings both inside and outside the
local church. We can act for God's glory, as part of
God's movement of transformation.

Such Spirited stewardship interweaves Christian
identity and ministry in our personal faith journeys and
in our congregational community life. It challenges us
to live out our covenant as a community of stewards
every day, not just on Sundays or in private.

Spirited stewardship embraces every dimension of
our living and turns the word *steward* into a verb. It
prompts us to express God's multifaceted relationship
with humanity in a myriad of creative ways.

Questions and Activities

- How might you see your local church's ministries from a mechanistic point of view? Write down your observations. Then list how you would see the congregation as a system. Find someone and compare your responses.
- Reflect on your personal journey so far as a steward for God. Where have you been in Egypt, and how has Egypt been inside you? What steps have you taken to risk going forward, and where do you find yourself now? What events or commitments have been turning points along the way? Do you have a vision of the promised land?
- What do your congregation's activities say about its identity? Does your church use its finances in a different way from the surrounding society? Do members know who receives the money they give for local, community, and global ministries? Do certain individuals or families have "a string on the balloon," able to pull the church's corporate plans in the direction of their personal dreams?

For Reflection

- Read the words of these hymns in *The United Methodist Hymnal:* "Take My Life, and Let It Be" (399); "Come, Thou Fount of Every Blessing" (400); "Of All the Spirit's Gifts to Me" (336). Write down your thoughts and feelings about phrases that speak to your life journey.

- Use this litany in your congregation. Prepare those present in advance for a gentle but honest time of confession and praise.

(Hold up a Bible.)
For your Living Word, O God, expressed uniquely through the Scriptures;
For your call to bring the good news to life by the living of our lives,
We thank you, God.

(Hold up a savings account book.)
For the times we have trusted in no one but ourselves;
For whenever we assume that our money belongs to us;
For the ways we have sought security in our financial assets and not in you;
Forgive us, O God.

(Hold up a personal calendar or planner.)
For the gift of time, when we seek to plan according to your priorities;
For when we are surprised by your presence and Word in unexpected places;
For quality time with those we love and with all those you love,
We thank you, God.

(Hold up a checkbook.)

For the way we have claimed to give our hearts to
   you but have held back our giving, afraid to give
   ourselves away;
For the times we've talked of changing our lives but
   have resisted losing any comfort in our lifestyle;
Forgive us, O God.

(Raise both hands.)
Hear the Word of new beginnings from God, the
giver of life and of every blessing: Our hands are
empty. Nothing belongs to us; everything we have
and are is a gift from God. This is good news! Our
hands are free of whatever things have bound us and
weighed us down, free now to receive and to share!
God owns and claims us in love and offers us a new
beginning, following God's presence and will. We
can begin anew, right now. **For this we praise God!**

Prayer
God of justice and compassion, thank you for every
gift of your grace! Guide us to see the gifts in others
and in ourselves and to encourage one another to
serve all your people. Help us glorify you in all things
through Jesus Christ, as stewards of your love. Amen.

Endnotes

1 See *Transforming Congregations for the Future*, by Loren B.
   Mead (The Alban Institute, 1994); pages 43, 53–61.
2 From "Creative Decision-Making," a workshop by Paul
   Dietterich of the Center for Parish Development, Sep-
   tember 1988.

3 See *The Crisis in the Churches: Spiritual Malaise, Fiscal Woe*, by Robert Wuthnow (Oxford University Press, 1997).

4 See *Leadership and the New Science: Learning About Organization From an Orderly Universe*, by Margaret Wheatley (Berrett-Koehler Publishers, Inc., 1992); pages 26–38.

CHAPTER TWO

God Is a Verb: Journeying Stewards in a Smoldering Wilderness

Burning Bushes

Moses hadn't exactly left Egypt under the best circumstances. Brought up as Egyptian in the royal household, he woke up to the shocking fact that he was Hebrew—economically oppressed, *in* but not *of* the society around him. One day, in a single explosive moment, Moses killed an Egyptian who had beaten a Hebrew. The next day Moses discovered that everyone knew about the covert murder. So he raced for the border (see Exodus 2:1-15).

On the day of Moses' encounter at the burning bush, he was living and working in Midian, where he had established a new life for himself. His life was not grand, but at least he was settled. A herder of sheep and goats in the wilderness, Moses had found a family connection and a territory that did not threaten his understanding of top-down power. While Pharaoh still ruled in Egypt, Moses could be a mini-pharaoh in the borderlands—in charge of the small bit his family owned, out of harm's way.

Pastors and church leaders today may feel like the pre-bush Moses. Most of us are not ex-murderers, but we know what it feels like to be on the downside of coercive power, whether at the hands of our jobs or of the church. We have found a place to work somewhere in the connection, and we're happy to mind our own business, tending our particular set of sheep and goats. We have stayed away from the visible centers of power—but the basic idea of ownership and of top-down authority still throbs in our hearts.

Real stewardship, however, is the opposite of ownership! It is all about receiving, using, and sharing resources *on behalf of* the Owner. And it doesn't work in a top-down way. That's the frustrating thing about it: it's like overlapping circles. God, the Artist and Owner of all, initiates an event out of love, justice, and grace. We dare to act on God's behalf, which sparks other God events. Our action also prompts responses by other daring stewards. Pretty soon God's initiative, our response, and our interactions with one another are all mixed up. No one can say clearly anymore which event comes as a top-down act of God and which comes from God's creative people. That's the Holy Spirit—always mixing things up.

So we return to Moses. Like the Hebrews that he later would lead, he was physically out of Egypt, but Egypt was still inside him. He thought he was running his own show (which many of us have thought, too, deep in our hearts).

But Moses ran into God. That's the tricky thing: even with the burning bush, God left it up to Moses to notice the something different in his landscape and then to decide whether or not to turn aside to check it out.

It takes a lot for us to turn aside. Something has to not fit, to strike a dissonant chord, for us to break with routine. If Egyptian illusions of our being in control of our lives and able to control others are working for us, we don't need to notice the bushes in the wilderness. In fact, we have to know first that we are in the wilderness before we can notice the bushes. We have to take time (whether by choice or not) to realize that something major is not working, or that things are working contrary to our assumptions about life. This recognition is the beginning of a paradigm shift, a way of viewing life that changes our whole sense of who we are (our identity) and also of what we are called to do (our ministry).

So that different bush caught Moses' attention (see Exodus 3:1-15). He noticed that the bush was not burning up, so he turned aside from whatever he had on his planner for that day to discover why the bush was on fire but still alive. The odd bush broke into Moses' awareness. God was already mixing up initiative and response. "When the LORD saw that he [Moses] had turned aside to see," says Exodus 3:4, then "God called to him out of the bush, 'Moses, Moses!'" God's personal call came only after God had gotten Moses' attention.

Moses' fiery encounter with God required him to increase his commitment by stages. First he was curious enough to turn aside. Next he decided to take a closer look. Then, when God called to him in that surprising event, Moses answered, "Here I am."

But God wasn't done yet. "Remove the sandals from your feet," God said, "for the place on which you are standing is holy ground." God established a place of holiness. Then (in case Moses hadn't gotten the full God-connection here) God said, "I am the God of your father, the God of Abraham, the God of Isaac, and the God of Jacob."

Here is the fire of God's call! Even before we hear God call our names, God invites us to see that the commonness of life is saturated with God's holiness. The Holy One whispers to us to turn aside, to enter into the Mystery that surrounds us, and to invest ourselves in the experience.

No part of our lives or of creation is too common or too unclean for God to be present. The entire earth is holy! Psalm 24:1 says, "The earth is the Lord's and all that is in it." All that lives upon, in, or above the earth belongs to God. This is the meaning of the Incarnation: God has come into human, creaturely existence—even to the least among us. God has made "every common bush afire with God!"

Moses trusted his experience, so he recognized the imprint of God's genuine presence. He hid his face, afraid to look directly at God. "I have observed the misery of my people who are in Egypt," God said. *Uh oh, Egypt!* thought Moses. *That's where I killed that taskmaster and buried him! I can't ever go back there again!*

"I have heard their cry on account of their taskmasters." *I knew it! The man I killed was a taskmaster. Now I'm in deep trouble!*

"Indeed,... I have come down to deliver them from the Egyptians, and to bring them up out of that land to a good and broad land." *Ah, at last! But how will you do that?*

"So come, I will send *you* to Pharaoh to bring my people, the Israelites, out of Egypt!"

We can imagine Moses' resistance, down to the set of his jaw and planting of his sturdy feet in the sandy soil. When he got over his shock, Moses had two main objections. First Moses asked, "Who am I that I should go to Pharaoh?"—as if God didn't remember that Moses was precisely the wrong person to ask Pharaoh for any favors. But God's answer was, "I will be with you." Oh, Moses considered. *Now that makes a difference. God will go with me!*

But then came Moses' second big objection: But who exactly are you? I don't even know your name! God answered, "I AM WHO I AM."

What's in a Name?

This divine name for God has tremendous implications. It does more than move beyond arguments about whether God is male or female (both begetting and giving birth). It breaks through bigger theistic boxes we have for our concept of God. God's personal name points to the vitality of what God does.

No wonder our own identity and ministry as the church cannot be separated, for we reflect the interlaced being and action of God! God brings into being all that was, is, and will be alive. We know God through what God does. This is God's dynamic presence, God's ongoing love-in-action.

So the question of our stewardship of what we actually do with the gospel—is a matter not just of our ministry, but also of our lives. Unless we remember God's dynamic love-inaction—the verbness of God—as the center of our identity, we risk losing the meaning and joy of who we are as human beings and as creatures on this earth.

Actions speak louder than words, not only for individuals but also for congregations. For example, in the spring of 1998, thirty thousand people worked as volunteers in forty-one programs offered by Glide Memorial United Methodist Church in San Francisco. The programs included opportunities to serve in an AIDS/HIV clinic, a computer learning center, and a drug recovery program. Volunteers also visited in hospitals and fed more than thirty-five hundred meals a day to the homeless.

Why did the congregation do all that? The Reverend Cecil Williams, Glide Memorial's pastor, said, "Too many people feel that they have to let it be known that they are Christian. You don't have to say it if you're a Christian. It's what you do."

Whatever the form of our ministries, Christianity is what we do because we know God by what God does. To look for God's presence in the world, we look for what God is doing. People know us as Christians in the same way, by looking at what we do. This God-is-a-verb understanding turns upside down our hierarchical view of a distant, royal deity who invites us to imitate its pharaoh-like dominion. It upends our old object-oriented view of stewardship that turns people creatures into tools and all that we have into assets to trade and abuse at will.

In the ancient world, every name had meaning and impact. People changed their names to reflect life-changing events. Magicians of that time assumed that knowing creatures' names brought control over them. But here at the burning bush, magic did not work for Moses. The name that God told Moses was God's "name forever" was YHWH (pronounced yah-way and sometimes written "Yahweh" in English).

This name is translated "the LORD" and "I AM WHO I AM" in most English Bibles. But *Yahweh* is not simply a name; it is a verb phrase that identifies Yahweh as one who is present and is the cause of all life. It is Yahweh who brings all things into being.[1]

Many Bible texts support this tie between God's name and actions and our own identity and behavior. God interacts with us and with all creation. For example, Psalm 81 calls us to remember an active God in the midst of God's people. Even the name of God recalls God's saving work at the Exodus and God's offer of guidance and nourishment since then. Psalm 148 tells us to live as expressions of praise and thanksgiving in the context of a grateful creation.

The Bible shows us that God's people have been and are on a journey of faith, and that God is One who goes with us. This belief in God's presence was the distinctive feature of what the ancient Hebrews called the God of their ancestors (see Exodus 3:13-16; 4:5). Other peoples in the ancient Near East understood their gods as connected to sacred places and bound by territorial boundaries. So when people left their homeland, they also left their gods. But the God of the Hebrews was attached not to a particular shrine or territory but rather to a people. What a revolutionary concept!

From the beginning the Hebrews believed that God traveled with them. This idea stands behind the tent of meeting. It was where "the Lorto used to speak to Moses face to face, as one speaks to a friend" (see Exodus 33:7-11; Deuteronomy 34:10).

Our traveling God also connects with the ark of the covenant, which Moses placed within the tent of meeting (see Exodus 40:1-3) and which Israel's leaders used well into King David's time (see Numbers 10:33-36; Joshua 3:3-6; 2 Samuel 6:1-5). The ark symbolized the presence of God, whom the Hebrews believed fought alongside their mortal warriors when they brought the ark into battle with them.

The theme of a God who journeys with us moves on into the Gospel of John, where the writer says, "And the Word became flesh and lived among us . . ." (John 1:14). The Greek term here for *lived* is derived from the same word as *tabernacle* or the *tent of meeting*, the place where God lived among the people of Israel. In the Old Testament the people carried the tabernacle with them on their journey. Today we might translate the word as "pitched a tent." In John, though, we learn that through Christ, we no longer need to carry an ark or a tent (tabernacle)—it is God who brings the tent to camp right along with us!

The Bible shows that action is essential not only to God but also to God's people. The Hebrew Scriptures speak of "the way" of Israel, referring to the people's way of living in the world. The Old Testament people saw the way of Israel on at least three levels: the destination toward which they traveled as a people (what we might call their goal or vision); the direction they chose (their basic lifestyle and ethics); and the way they walked (their particular lifestyle and personality as a community in the world).

The early Christians continued this sense of momentum. One of the initial names for the early Christians was people of "the Way" (Acts 9:2; 19:9, 23; 22:4). The phrase referred to the way they lived as well as the way of Christ, the direction they had chosen.

So why talk about God's journeying with us and our way of going? Such a discussion shows the interrelatedness between who God is and God's activity, and between who we are and what we do. Just as the Book of James says that works must accompany faith (James 2:14-26), so our ministry and identity are essential to each other.

Jesus went even deeper with this interrelationship between God and ourselves, between being and action. In John 14:10-12 Jesus suggests that God acts through us as we dare to act for God. This is the dynamic of stewarding the gospel—when we do something on God's behalf, trusting that God the Initiator will work through us and through others by sheer grace! Jesus goes even further when he says that the one who believes in him will not only do the works that he does but also "will do greater works than these" (John 14:12)!

Ephesians 3 echoes Jesus' statement that we will do great things, thanks to the One "who by the power at work within us is able to accomplish abundantly far more than all we can ask or imagine" (verses 20-21)! Our actions grow out of our "inner being," the writer says, as Christ dwells in our hearts and we are "rooted and grounded in love" (verses 16 and 17). Just as trees grow only to the extent that their roots deepen, so our lives grow only to the extent that we are rooted in God's love. God created us to be stewards of the gospel. Whether for good or for ill, we all live from the inside out. We act out of the inner truth of who we are and to whom we belong.

Walkin' the Talk

What's important, Jesus says, is not to simply cry out "Lord! Lord!" but to obey him. The one who acts upon Jesus' words is like a homeowner who builds a house upon rock, not sand (Matthew 7:24-27). We can't take anything in life for granted! As with a physical earthquake or flood, unless we have a spiritually solid ground of trust in God, the faith upon which we've stood for years may suddenly shift under our feet, thrusting up a whole new reality that we must deal with, like it or not.

Moses must have felt exactly this kind of earthquake. He stood before the burning bush, hearing God's call to return to Egypt with a seemingly impossible task.

As with Moses, so with us. A day has leapt upon us, whether we're ready or not. Stark challenges confront us. Will we continue to "do church" and "do stewardship" in the old, pharaoh-like way? Or will we see ourselves as stewards of God's subtle but explosive flames burning around and even through us?

The Stewardship Thread

Moses isn't the only example of God's call to stewardship. A thread of stewardship weaves throughout the Bible, reflecting a growing concept. In the Old Testament the steward had a close relationship with the owner and was empowered to act as that person's representative. The steward could have major responsibilities. Abraham even sent Eliezer, his chief steward, to a foreign country to bring back a wife for Abraham's son,

Isaac (Genesis 24). Likewise, Joseph became Pharaoh's steward over all of Egypt, managing the entire country's economy (Genesis 41:25-57).

Old Testament stewards discerned, as trustees, the best course of action for the family or nation. They were not always good stewards, however. For example, Shebna was the head of King Hezekiah's government, but he used his power to increase his own wealth and influence. God kicked him out of office and publicly shamed him for his greed (Isaiah 22:15-25).

In the New Testament, stewardship weaves an even richer fabric of meanings. Trusteeship shifts to partnership. Paul says we are "God's servants, working together" (1 Corinthians 3:9). As partners, we are to work together for a common purpose, to bring human-ity into communion with God (Ephesians 1:3-13).

Likewise, New Testament stewards are managers of the church. Jesus entrusts us to run the household of God on his behalf (Luke 12:41-48). At the same time, Jesus is our model as the authentic steward of God's grace. His service, done out of willingness, not servi-tude, becomes the ultimate form of greatness. So too with us. Jesus tells us, "The last will be first, and the first will be last" (Matthew 20:16). He redefines leadership as taking a serving role (Mark 10:42-45). In complete obedience as God's steward, Jesus stands as our primary model for life, leadership, and service.

Paul tells us that the Spirit leads us into even more than being God's partners. God brings us all the way into God's family, adopted as full sons and daughters, through the Spirit (Romans 8:14-17; Ephesians 1:4).

Divine Partnership

The shape of this good news has distinctive facets, which we discover in the word *koinonia*. *Koinonia* is sometimes translated as fellowship or sharing. But the term actually means something more inclusive, intimate, and intensive. *Koinonia* specifically enriches our understanding of stewardship. Paul uses *koinonia* to convey a particular relationship with Jesus (as in 1 Corinthians 1:9), with the gospel (as in Philippians 1:3-5), with the poor (as in Romans 15:26), and with members of the Christian community (2 Corinthians 9:13). In Philemon verse 6, when Paul pleads for the life of Philemon's runaway slave, he speaks of *koinonia* quality. He says, "I pray that the sharing [*koinonia*] of your faith may become effective when you perceive all the good that we may do for Christ."

At least three things are striking about the word *koinonia*. First, it describes the vital dynamic of partnership in the gospel. In Philippians 1:3-5, Paul writes, "I thank my God every time I remember you... because of your sharing [*koinonia*] in the gospel from the first day until now." This partnership includes all aspects of our life and witness as a community of faith.

Second, while *koinonia* connotes spiritual unity, it is also immensely economic. In 2 Corinthians 9:13, Paul speaks of the Christians' offerings as coming out of "the generosity of your sharing [*koinonia*] with them [the poor] and with all others." Acts 2:42-47 describes the early Christian community, connecting their sense of unity with how they managed their possessions and property to benefit the needs of the members. Throughout the Book of Acts, *koinonia* emphasizes the Christians' common witness in practical ways and also connotes holding things in common.

Third, *koinonia* expresses the mutuality of giving and receiving. In Romans 15:25-27, for example, Paul invites the Roman church to join with the Christians of Macedonia and Achaia in the offering to help the Jerusalem Christians respond to victims of famine in their region (see 2 Corinthians 8 and 9). Paul tells the Romans it is a matter of sharing material and spiritual blessings. Jerusalem gave the spiritual gift of the gospel through Jesus; the Gentile churches can give the material blessing of money to feed those who are starving. Paul says the Macedonian and Achaian Christians are making contributions—*koinonia*—for the Jerusalem poor.

Given the depth and associations of this word *koinonia*, we can translate the word as stewardship. It describes a community's way of living as well as a personal relationship with Jesus. It links spiritual and material gifts and describes a corporate lifestyle of practical action and advocacy. It is a constantly-changing dynamic of receiving and giving, a partnership in the gospel that results in practical economic and lifestyle relationships, in action for and with others on Christ's behalf.

Stewards of God's Grace

First Peter 4:10-11 tells us, "Like good stewards of the manifold grace of God, serve one another with whatever gift each of you has received … so that God may be glorified in all things through Jesus Christ."

God's grace comes in unique forms to us, fitted to who we are with our personal bundles of neuroses, gifts, and eccentricities. This grace touches people differently in various times, cultures, and places. Yet it is the same grace of God that shines through us all.

In this particular moment we may find ourselves barefoot and trembling before a specific burning bush. Our jaws drop in surprise. God has our attention. We are stewards of God's manifold grace. But how will we live out our stewardship?

Questions and Activities

- What "burning bush" nudges you to believe that God is calling you or your congregation to do things differently as stewards of the gospel?
- Do you identify in any way with the pre-bush Moses, such as in his views of power or of self-sufficiency? How is Egypt still inside of you? How does the Bible's stewardship thread challenge these early-Moses perceptions?

- What could *koinonia* stewardship look like in your church and community?
- "Lift Every Voice and Sing," Hymn No. 32 in *Songs of Zion* (Abingdon, 1981), talks about suffering and God's presence on our journey as God's people. How does this fit with "the way of Israel," "the way of Christ," your faith journey, and the faith journey of your community?
- "Altar on Mt. Moriah," Hymn No. 57 in *Hymns From the Four Winds: A Collection of Asian American Hymns* (Abingdon Press, 1983), speaks of three mountains where God gave three great gifts. On Mt. Moriah, God offered a ram in place of Abraham's son Isaac. On Mt. Carmel, God gave fire, then rain to end the people's famine. And on the Mount of Calvary, Jesus shed his blood to save the world. On what "mountain" have you experienced God's overwhelming gift of grace? What difference has it made in your life?

Suggestion for Meditation

The third verse of "Immortal, Invisible, God Only Wise" (*The United Methodist Hymnal*, 103) declares:

> To all, life thou givest, to both great and small;
> in all life thou livest, the true life of all;
> we blossom and flourish as leaves on the tree,
> and wither and perish, but naught changeth thee.

Recall your memories of endings and new beginnings, your experiences of God in the great and small aspects of living. What does God call you to express through your living?

Endnotes

1 See *Canaanite Myth and Hebrew Epic: Essays in the History of the Religion of Israel*, by Frank Moore Cross (Harvard University Press, 1973); pages 60-75.

CHAPTER THREE

❈

Stewards of God's Mysteries: Reflecting the Activity of God

Many have stood before God to answer a steward's call. While our current encounter is unique, the trembling faithful of many generations have stood in this place in their time—Jews of the prophets' era, trinitarian Christians of all persuasions, and United Methodists of our age and other generations. God acts through people who are stewards, including Moses, John Wesley, and us.

Judaism is a living world religion, but it is also a part of our Christian tradition. Christians believe that Jesus fulfilled the Hebrew Scripture as the Messiah or Christ, the Anointed One who makes visible God's reign on earth. So before exploring four Christian traditions related to stewardship, we note two dimensions of biblical Hebrew faith. One is obeying God's law

(*mitzvot*) in all that we do; the other is repairing the
world (*tikkun olam*).

Mitzvot

For Jews, *mitzvot* are the commandments of God made
real in human lives. They range from observing the sab-
bath to teaching children about Passover and giving
money to the poor. For non-Orthodox Jews, these commandments are occasions for choice. They are like jewels embedded in a path; one must choose which to dig
up to carry along the way.[1] All together, the *mitzvot* rep-
resent a way of life that tries to transform nearly every
human action into a means of communion with God.

One *mitzvah* is that of *tzedakah*, which means
"righteous giving." In Jewish tradition, the norm is ten
percent of a family's income. " *Tzedakah* is misnamed
when we call it charity," says Rabbi Greg Wolfe of California, "because people give not out of personal empa-
thy but rather out of obligation to do the right thing."
Such *tzedakah* giving generally involves the donation of
money.

Each year Rabbi Wolfe's Beth Haverim congregation celebrates Mitzvah Day, when children and adults
alike choose projects to help the community. In 1999
they gave blood, worked at a battered-women's shelter,
donated items to people with AIDS, visited people who
were isolated and limited in their ability to leave home,
worked in the local arboretum, called on retirement-

home residents, and provided childcare—all with an energized, upbeat spirit.

While there are 613 commandments in the Torah (the first five books of the Bible), Micah reduced them to three: do justice, love kindness, and walk humbly with your God (Micah 6:8). Amos and Habakkuk each reduced them to one. Amos said, "Seek me [God] and live" (Amos 5:4). Habakkuk said, "The righteous live by their faith" (Habakkuk 2:4).[2]

Jesus reduced the *mitzvot* to two inseparable commandments: "'You shall love the Lord your God with all your heart, and with all your soul, and with all your mind.' This is the greatest and first commandment. And a second is like it: 'You shall love your neighbor as yourself.' On these two commandments hang all the law and the prophets" (Matthew 22:37-40).

Vacaville St. Paul's United Methodist Church and Vacaville Faith United Methodist Fellowship, two sixty-member congregations, take Jesus' statement to heart. They meet together regularly for a "Second Commandment Group." In these gatherings, they explore God's call to express love for neighbor and world. One person finds God's call in public-school teaching, another in work with Habitat for Humanity, and another in advocacy for global political issues and participation in the local church's weekly food distribution.

It's no surprise that these activities evoke images of action and of fire. At Pentecost, the event that birthed the church, the Holy Spirit acted upon Jesus' followers like non-consuming fire that rested on each one of them (Acts 2:3). In that moment, God's living presence transformed them and thrust them into action as a new people. Their terror turned to boldness. They left their locked room and rushed into the streets to tell those whom they had feared what God had done through Jesus Christ. Empowered personally by the flames of the Spirit, they offered a life-changing corporate witness that spread like wildfire on the earth.

We help spread the flames when we act on our faith as part of God's community in the world. And the heart of it depends upon our personal relationship with the One who creates, redeems, and sustains us with every breath of our lives.

Repairing the World

The second aspect of Judaism to enrich our Christian stewardship is *tikkun olam*, "repairing the world." It calls us to care for God's creation and for the human relationships with which God has gifted us.

As the concept of *tikkun olam* developed over the centuries, it became a rationale for social action on behalf of society at large. It reminds us that human beings have an important role in realizing God's plan for the world. In fact, we are partners with God in the process of repair. God is not merely the sponsor for our daily acts of reparation. Rather, God chooses to complete the original design for creation through our partnership with God, as we put back into order the fragmented pieces of created life.

Gershom Scholem, a Jewish scholar, says the chasm between God and ourselves can be mended only by studying Torah (God's law or teaching), by following *mitzvot*, and by bathing our lives in prayer. He describes *tikkun* (repairing) as humanity's task on earth and as our highest ideal.[3] He calls it "striving for the perfection of the world," the restoration of God's original aim for creation.[4]

One synagogue, congregation Beth El in Sudbury, Massachusetts, invites its members to repair the world as a congregation. In 1998, after a *Tikkun Olam* survey and individual interviews, the congregation sponsored a meeting with state legislators over community issues, including women's access to local health clinics. At the same time, the synagogue launched a yearlong program of service projects. Members of all ages gathered books for school children and clothes for families in women's shelters, planted and weeded around a house for recovering alcoholics and their families, studied the prayer book, and supported an area-wide literacy campaign.

The Hebrew *tikkun olam* reminds Christians of two essential dimensions of stewardship—caring for the earth itself and repairing relationships as part of God's human family.

Stewardship of the Earth

We can encourage good stewardship of the earth in
many ways. The following are some examples that your
congregation can use.

1. Host a "Creation Awareness Conference" for
your area. In an interdenominational event using religious and economic experts, church leaders learn to
lead their congregations in responsible environmental
stewardship, including the areas of preaching in an
ecological context, sustainable living, corporate agri-
culture in your state or province, and gardening and
gleaning programs.

2. Sponsor a "Lord's Acre" program linked to biblical foundations such as Exodus 34:22-26; Leviticus 23;
and Deuteronomy 12:6. The Lord's Acre can take different forms. For example, four congregations in rural
northeast Texas hold an annual Thanksgiving festival.
Members display raw produce as well as canned and pre-
served goods. With missionaries as guest speakers, they
join in worship and give a major financial offering to a
designated global project

3. Hold the "Lord's Hour," when people offer
their abilities and efforts for others. The following have
all been offered as "first fruits": a six-year-old boy
brought a row of potatoes he had grown and offered
them for auction; a barber donated a year's worth of
haircuts to the highest bidder; a mechanic donated a
brake job; a farmer dedicated the yield from an acre of
corn; a couple who owned a dairy offered a bed-and-

breakfast weekend to an urban family who bid the most; a woman gave a catered candlelight dinner for two.

These efforts were stewardship, not fundraising, according to Melvin West, editor of the *United Methodist Rural Fellowship Bulletin*. The focus was to encourage Christians to understand their unique, God-given gifts and then express their gratitude by offering the "fruits" of those gifts to God through others.[5]

4. Have a "Talent Share Fair" and worship. Participants bring something that shows how God has gifted them in a special way, such as music, artwork, garden produce, baked goods, woodwork, stitchery, field crops, animals (or photos of them), or pictures of children.

5. Develop a community garden or church-based gardening project. For example, five churches in Michigan have planted gardens since 1980. The produce from these gardens goes to Neighborhood Houses in inner-city sections of Flint, Detroit, and Pontiac.

6. Study stewardship of the earth in your local church, using such resources as *101 Ways to Help Save the Earth*, by the National Council of the Churches of Christ in the USA; *God's Earth, Our Home*, edited by Shantilal P. Bhagat; *Hope for the Earth: A Handbook for Christian Environmental Groups*, by Sharon Delgado; *Hope for the Land: Nature in the Bible*, by Richard Cartwright Austin; *It's God's World: Christians, the Environment, and Climate Change*, by Vera K. White; and *Reclaiming America: Restoring Nature to Culture*, by Richard Cartwright Austin.

7. Arrange a "Toxic Tour" to see firsthand how your community deals with pollution. Set up a panel of area experts to discuss pollution dangers and emerging community solutions.

8. Observe Rural Life Sunday in worship, or celebrate the United Nations' yearly Earth Day.

9. Set up a monthly letter-writing table after worship for people to correspond with legislators about issues affecting local or global agricultural systems, the environment, and long-term effects of food and work practices.

Stewardship of Relationships

Relationships are a channel to help repair the world. We don't "manage" the relationships God gives us, as if we were in control. Rather, as faithful stewards we focus on the Spirit's presence and movement among us. In this way our relationships can grow with God's guidance, reflecting God's self-giving love in the quality of our care for one another.

But relationships are not only one-on-one. They are also part of economic, social, and political systems. In these larger systems good stewards become partners in repairing fragmented community. For example, in 1999 when two young men opened fire on other students at Columbine High School in Littleton, Colorado, area congregations immediately went to work. Staff members from Columbine United Church (a three-denomination ministry) drove to the school to help move students to safety. The district superintendent set up a network of area pastors to provide counseling, supported by the conference youth coordinator and crisis counselors from the United Methodist Committee on Relief. Six nearby United Methodist congregations scheduled prayer services throughout that week, and the conference treasurer set up an account to receive contributions to assist students' families.[6]

Caution: God at Work

When most people say the words *Holy Spirit*, they're talking about a subjective experience—a certain feeling of God's presence or assurance. But for the Cappadocians, the Holy Spirit was an objective reality: the fact of God as the Source of all life in creation and in human history.[7]

Why care about the Cappadocians? Because they affirmed the Holy Spirit as God and formulated the language of the Trinity that the global church accepted at the first Council of Constantinople in A.D. 381. The Cappadocians were Basil of Caesarea (St. Basil the Great), Gregory of Nazianzus, and St. Gregory of Nyssa. They grounded their understanding of the Holy Spirit not in who God *is* (God's essence), but in what God *does* (God's activity in the world).

What has this to do with us? Plenty! When we hear the name *Holy Spirit* today, we're apt to think of a static, often empty category that's part of a formula we learned in Sunday school. It does not necessarily affect our lives in any particular way.

But what if the Holy Spirit is the dynamic activity of God, not only in our personal lives or even in our congregation but also in all human history and throughout creation? What if the Holy Spirit is the God who brings us to the reign of heaven, returns us to adoption as God's children, and makes it possible for us to share in Christ's grace?

What if the Holy Spirit is not who God *is*, some distant deity, but what God is *doing* all around us? If we focus on God's activity, we can see God's active involvement all around us as God's fire upon the earth!

What does this have to do with stewardship? A lot! When we are faithful, joyous stewards of the gospel, we reflect God's activity in the way we live our lives. Instead of being defined by what we believe, we are defined by how we live, by the One whom we follow. And that makes all the difference in the world.

The Ways of Love

While contemporary lovers count the many ways they love their partners, Christians discover God's love and ask, "How does God love me? Let me count the ways!" Perhaps another word for stewardship is love—God's love working upon and through human beings. This understanding of stewardship gives additional meaning to the term *incarnation*. *Incarnation* refers to Jesus as God's Word Incarnate, literally enfleshed on earth.

But it can also refer to Jesus' followers, who incarnate God's love, giving it life through their loving actions.

The Incarnation is God's grace at work. We experience this grace through God's activity all around us, finding evidence of what God is doing in whatever is life-giving (God's creating love), whatever is life-saving (God's redeeming love), and whatever is life-fulfilling (God's empowering love).[8]

This understanding of Incarnation is the mystery of the Trinity! It invites us to start not with "Who is God?" but with "What's happening in life? Where do we sense God at work?" And because we start with God's actions, not God's essence, we can participate as Christ's body in action. It's not just that God has given us individual spiritual gifts to share, but that Christian community itself is a gift. It makes a difference not only in how we live, but that we live at all.

There's more. Not only is Christian community a gift; it is also part of the arena in which God as Creator, God as Christ, and God as Holy Spirit relate to one another! The dynamics of God interact within human relationships. Leonardo Boff says we can follow the model of the Trinity itself in how we work together as Christian communities. He says that the nature of the Trinity is the exuberance of God's inner life in communion, in *koinonia* with one another. This internal union sheds light on our own existence and tells us the ultimate structure of human life.[9]

Stewardship and the Means of Grace

Any activity can become what John Wesley calls a means of grace—a channel for God's action in the world, a way in which God works in and upon our lives. For Wesley the means of grace are both the context within which we live as Christians and the process by which we maintain our love of God and neighbor. They are not only settings in which to act but also ways we learn to respond to God as responsible stewards. When we share in Holy Communion, for example, or feed and clothe the poor, God not only calls us to put love into action but also empowers us to be capable of such love.

But we can go one step further. The means of grace provide an internal mutuality, where God's grace and our response interweave to form the fabric of our spiritual lives.[10] If stewardship is whatever we do with the gospel, then it is not merely a series of external actions. Stewardship becomes a way of life, flowing out from our hearts into daily action, our faithful behavior reinforcing our faith.

General Means of Grace

For Wesley the means of grace are not only actions and practices but also attitudes. Grace comes to and through us when we seek to deny ourselves, to obey God completely, to keep all the commandments, to be attentive, to take up our cross daily, and to exercise the presence of God.

As with the *mitzvot* in Judaism, the Christian means of grace invite us to participate in an ongoing relationship with God. Here again is the internal mutuality of stewardship, where God's initiative both prompts us to respond and empowers our response.

Instituted Means of Grace

The instituted means of grace are specific acts of worship and discipline that belong to the church in all times and cultures. For Wesley, the greatest of these are prayer, searching the Scriptures, and Holy Communion.

To John Wesley, prayer is "the breath of our spiritual life."[11] We can pray without ceasing, using the Lord's Prayer as a pattern for our focus. Prayer invites us into an intentional relationship with God, prepares us to receive God's gifts, and shapes the way we act in response to God."[12]

Wesley believed that the heart of Christian life comes through searching the Scriptures, both in our personal reading and by listening to sermons. We are to bathe our Scripture reading in prayer for the Spirit to guide us. We can examine ourselves by what we read and hear. Through this means, God increases our wisdom.

Wesley saw frequent Holy Communion as essential to preparation for God's grace. The act brings together past, present, and future as we recall Jesus' saving death, expect his personal presence, and anticipate his return in glory. Communion invites people to faith and deepens their love for God and neighbor. It prompts gratitude as a natural response to the remembrance of God's sacrificial love celebrated in the service of Holy Communion."[13]

In addition to these three major means of grace, Wesley also urged fasting to aid prayer and bodily health, to express sorrow for sin, to avoid excessive consumption, and to increase one's love of God. Likewise, he saw Christian conferencing as important to Christian life, in intentional conversations among Christians and in the *koinonia* of believers gathered together. Wesley's particular structure of Christian conferencing developed in classes and bands.

Prudential Means of Grace

Prudential means of God's grace are those practices that vary with the occasion. Among these are "works of mercy," or particular acts of holy living. These actions are not only channels for God's grace to work upon us, but also ends in themselves as expressions of love. They reveal faithful stewardship of both personal and systemic relationships, including Wesley's opposition to slavery and advocacy for the poor.

For Wesley, solidarity with the poor and outcasts came squarely out of the gospel. He believed that "outreach to the poor is the litmus test of . . . honest stewardship."[14] (See "Wesley as Steward," on page 70.)

Alongside work with the poor came visiting the sick and imprisoned. The first Methodists held regular worship in two prisons, leading semi-weekly prayers, preaching on Sundays, and offering monthly Holy Communion. They set aside money to pay the prisoners' debts and to buy them medicine, books, and legal advice.

What Wesley called the General Rules are still part of our doctrine and discipline.[15] Two of these prudential means of grace are to do no harm and to do all the good you can. "Doing no harm" means specific attentiveness to avoiding evil, including practices that can destroy indirectly. For example, Wesley advised not only against drunkenness but also against buying or selling alcohol, not only against quarreling but also against unprofitable conversation. He opposed not only conspicuous consumption but also the accumulation of goods, and advocated pooling personal economic resources as a measure of Christian life.

"Doing good" means taking specific positive actions. Wesley included daily habits of industry, frugality, community participation, and hands-on involvement with the poor.

Other prudential means of grace were specific ordinances of God, such as prayer meetings, Watch Night services, love feasts, and covenant renewal worship. John Wesley used what became the Covenant Renewal Service on August 11, 1755. Today, United Methodist churches often celebrate the Covenant Renewal Service on New Year's Eve or on the first Sunday in January. Its Covenant Prayer (printed at the end of this chapter) remains a powerful personal statement of obedience to God.

The distinctive expression of early Methodism was John Wesley's system of societies, classes, and bands. He began organizing Methodist Societies for groups of individuals "to pray together, to receive the word of exhortation, and to watch over one another in love, that they might help each other to work out their salvation."[16] When the Bristol Society grew to one thousand members, they devised a plan for helping pay off the building debt. The society divided into classes of twelve, each with a leader. The leader visited class members weekly to collect a penny from each to help pay off the debt. In the process, leaders began detecting members who were not living by the Methodist disciplines. Soon Wesley realized the potential for the classes and changed their focus from collecting money to identifying members who were slipping from their Christian ways, with the intent of helping such members turn back to Christian living. Copying Bristol's pattern, he formed weekly class meetings in other societies as they grew.

As the classes flourished, some members wanted an opportunity for more intensive experience of mutual confession and forgiveness. So Wesley formed smaller bands of six to eight persons each. Wesley set up separate bands for penitents (those who had fallen away) to recover their former spiritual ground.

He also created a select society for the spiritually mature who wished to "press after perfection."[17] It was in the select society that Wesley said he felt he could "unbosom myself on all occasions, without reserve."[18] Each member agreed to keep the group's conversations in full confidence and to "bring, once a week, all he can spare toward a common stock."[19] This sharing of resources was the most complete realization of the

Christian life, a recovery of the Christian experience in Acts 2, and a down payment on the coming reign of God. As such, it promoted an alternative social and economic order within the larger English society.[20]

All these means of grace wove themselves together to form a strong fabric of personal and corporate stewardship—a way for the early Methodists to live out the gospel. The General Rules in *The Book of Discipline of The United Methodist Church* (pages 59–74) area link between our early Methodist roots and contemporary commitments of The United Methodist Church.

Wesley as Steward

John Wesley's own life also gives us a powerful model of the practice of stewardship. We can learn from his

• **Stewardship of the gospel**—Wesley's primary task was clear. His ministry suggests that whenever he faced a crossroads, his basic question was, Does it bring people to faith? If the answer was yes, he was willing to change his methods. For example, on one occasion when he heard that a layman was preaching, he intended to stop it, insisting that only clergy were authorized to preach. But his mother urged him to listen to the man and decide for himself. As a result, lay preaching became one of the hallmark gifts of Methodism to the world.

Likewise, George Whitefield persuaded Wesley to preach outside the church pulpit. Once Wesley realized how many more people could come to faith, he began to preach on street corners and in open fields. In this way he reached an economic class of people who were not welcome in the established churches but were hungry to hear the good news.

• **Priorities**—Wesley considered visiting the sick and the poor a "matter of absolute duty," since "these are the marks whereby the Shepherd of Israel will know and judge his sheep at the great day."[21] He often invited them to eat at "the Foundery" [sic] and even begged for money on their behalf. He spent a meager thirty pounds a year on himself, and gave any surplus of his income to the poor.

Wesley also established advocacy for the poor as a priority among the Methodists. He was clear on his call as evangelist to the poor and the disinherited. For Wesley, the entire Methodist mission might be summarized as preaching good news to the poor. He asserted that religion should begin where God begins: with the poor, the despised, the oppressed, and those on the margins. He founded self-help organizations, including clinics, cooperatives, and credit unions. He said that trying to acquire more than what is strictly necessary is robbing from the poor. He urged people to recognize that their claims to the earth's resources must be based on their concern for the needs of their neighbor.

• **Use of money**—Wesley preached, "Gain all you can," "save all you can," "give all you can."[22] He meant going beyond giving a tithe, a fifth, one-half, or even three-quarters of one's income. His rule was first to provide only what is needed for oneself and one's household; second, to do good for those in the household of faith; and third, to help all people. In this way, he said, "You render unto God the things that are God's, not only by what you give to the poor, but also by that which you expend in providing things needful for yourself and your household."[23]

• **Use of time**—As with money, so with time. Methodists were to waste nothing. Wesley believed that "redeeming the time" (Ephesians 5:16, King James Version) means "saving all the time you can for the best purposes," taking it away from "sloth, ease, pleasure, worldly business," and even excess sleep.[24]

While at Oxford, the exacting time schedules of Wesley's friends earned them the mocking term *Methodists*. They arose early every morning, studied theology and the classics together in the evening, visited prisoners once or twice a week, spent one or two hours weekly visiting the poor, and fasted twice a week. They resolved to plan every conversation beforehand so that it would be useful. Wesley also spent several hours a day reading Scripture.

Wesley's historical ordination questions reflect a strict stewardship of time. One question asks, "Are you determined to employ all your time in the work of God?" Others say, "Be diligent. Never be unemployed. Never be triflingly employed. Never trifle away time; neither spend any more time at any one place than is strictly necessary. Be punctual."[25] Effective use of time continues Wesley's legacy.

A Spirited Heritage

When we say yes to becoming God's stewards, we are not alone. We have a living tradition of Spirit-centered stewardship from which we can draw. Judaism teaches us two central aspects of biblical faith: the *mitzvot* (commandments, including selfless giving) and repairing the world (care for God's creation and for human relationships). Our core Christian belief in the Holy Spirit points us to God's activity around, in, and even through us. And the Trinity describes the mystery of God's love-in-action, which we seek to reflect in our lives.

Further, United Methodists find a powerful example of stewardship in John Wesley's means of grace. We discover a model of good stewardship in Wesley's own life: in his primary task, his priority with the poor, his use of money, and his stewardship of time.

But one question remains. Given the challenges now before us—the depth of biblical stewardship and of God's call, and such a strong heritage of Spirited stewardship—now what do we do?

Questions and Activities

- What specific activities, like the Jews' *mitzvot*, have become jewels along your path?
- How can you participate more fully in "repairing the world"?

- How can the understanding of Trinity as God's activity in the world reshape and deepen your sense of community and of stewardship?
- What means of grace have become important to you personally? In what ways can they strengthen your personal stewardship of the gospel?
- Think about your congregation as a community of stewards. What is the *why* that empowers and inspires your church family, even as you struggle with the *how* of embodying it?

For Reflection

- "Jesus Christ, Workers' Lord" is Hymn No. 71 in *Hymns From the Four Winds: A Collection of Asian American Hymns* (Abingdon Press, 1983). It talks about how human labor joins with God's gifts to bring the fruits of love, and describes the human family as partners who share the earth. When have you seen this quality of working together? How can your church become a catalyst for such a partnership?
- Read the words to the following hymns in *The United Methodist Hymnal*. Write down what the phrases of these hymns evoke in your life: "Bois la Semilla" (583); "Forth in Thy Name, O Lord" (438); "Whom Shall I Send?" (582).

Prayer

Say the heart of John Wesley's Covenant Prayer.

> I am no longer my own, but thine.
> Put me to what thou wilt, rank me with whom
>   thou wilt.
> Put me to doing, put me to suffering.
> Let me be employed by thee or laid aside for thee,
> exalted for thee or brought low by thee.
> Let me be full, let me be empty.
> Let me have all things, let me have nothing.
> I freely and heartily yield all things
> to thy pleasure and disposal.[26]

Endnotes

1   See *Living Judaism: The Complete Guide to Jewish Belief, Tradition, and Practice*, by Rabbi Wayne Dosick (HarperSanFrancisco, 1995); page 34.

2   See *Judaism*, edited by Arthur Hertzberg (George Braziller, 1962); pages 72–73.

3   See *Major Trends in Jewish Mysticism*, by Gershom G. Scholem (Schocken Books, 1941); pages 233–234.

4   See *Major Trends in Jewish Mysticism*, by Gershom G. Scholem (Schocken Books, 1941); page 246. This phrase sounds similar to John Wesley's question of those to be ordained, "Are you going on to perfection?" Wesley's question stood squarely upon the basis of God's prevenient, pardoning, and nurturing grace.

5   See "The Lord's Acre/Hour Program: The Basics," by Mel West, in *United Methodist Rural Fellowship Bulletin*, Spring 1998; pages 8–9.

6   As reported by United Methodist News Service, April 21, 1999.

7 See *Toward a Contemporary Theology of the Holy Spirit: An Inquiry Into the Thought of Wolfhart Pannenberg and John B. Cobb*, by Inagrace Dietterich (The University of Chicago, 1987). A Doctor of Philosophy dissertation; pages 3–7.

8 See *In Trust: A Comprehensive Process for Cultivating Christian Stewardship*, by Paul M. Dietterich and Inagrace T. Dietterich (The Center for Parish Development, 1984); pages 20–21.

9 See *Trinity and Society*, by Leonardo Boff, translated by Paul Burns (Orbis Books, 1988).

10 For examples of this internal mutuality, see the following writings of John Wesley: Sermon 22, "Upon Our Lord's Sermon on the Mount, Discourse II," on "Blessed are the merciful"; Sermon 23, "Upon Our Lord's Sermon on the Mount, Discourse III," on love of God, neighbor, and self; and "A Plain Account of Christian Perfection" on holiness of heart and life, which describes works of piety and works of mercy as inseparable.

11 From *Explanatory Notes Upon the New Testament*, by John Wesley; notes on 1 Thessalonians 5:16-18.

12 Discussed in *The Presence of God in the Christian Life: John Wesley and the Means of Grace*, by Henry H. Knight, III (The Scarecrow Press, Inc., 1992); pages 117–118.

13 See *The Presence of God in the Christian Life: John Wesley and the Means of Grace*, by Henry H. Knight, III (The Scarecrow Press, Inc., 1992); page 141.

14 From "Good News to the Poor in the Wesleyan Heritage," by Theodore W. Jennings, Jr., in *Theology and Evangelism in the Wesleyan Heritage*, edited by James C. Logan (Kingswood Books, 1994); page 149.

15 See "Doctrine and Discipline in the Christian Life," in *The Book of Discipline of The United Methodist Church-1996*

(The United Methodist Publishing House, 1996); page 46.

16 From "A Plain Account of the People Called Methodists," by John Wesley.

17 From "A Plain Account of the People Called Methodists," by John Wesley.

18 From "A Plain Account of the People Called Methodists," by John Wesley.

19 From "A Plain Account of the People Called Methodists," by John Wesley.

20 Discussed in The Presence of God in the Christian Life: John Wesley and the Means of Grace, by Henry H. Knight, III (The Scarecrow Press, Inc., 1992); page 103.

21 From "Letters from the Reverend John Wesley to Various Persons, CCLXXIII—To the Same, December 10, 1777," by John Wesley.

22 From Sermon 50, "The Use of Money," by John Wesley. See also Sermon 87, "The Danger of Riches," by John Wesley.

23 From Sermon 87, "The Danger of Riches," by John Wesley.

24 From Sermon 93, "On Redeeming the Time," by John Wesley.

25 From The Book of Discipline of The United Methodist Church-1996 (The United Methodist Publishing House, 1996); paragraph 321.4.d.

26 From The United Methodist Hymnal (The United Methodist Publishing House, 1989); 607.

CHAPTER FOUR

❖

Stewards in Action: The Journey is our Home

Stewardship is an ongoing journey. There are several approaches with which we can begin a lifelong process to deepen our commitment and willingness to act upon it. We can begin by examining our ways of worship and our commitments to giving.

Embodying Our Worship

Spirited stewardship embodies our worship of God so that it flows out from the heart of Sunday congregational worship. The offering can be the highlight of worship, as we give God all that we are. Worshipers may offer quilts or crafts to donate through the church, hours of community volunteer service, offertory music or liturgical movement, or time and dedication to work as vacation Bible school helpers. Three farmers in

Nebraska knew that their grain wouldn't sell until later, but they wanted to give God the first of the crop. So they put the scale ticket from their first truckload of corn into the offering plate. In Pennsylvania a young man offered one day a month to do custodial work at the church.[1] When people give such a range of offerings, the financial secretary can list in the bulletin what was offered to God the previous week, thereby sparking more creative ideas.

Stewardship also naturally flows out of journaling about our individual spiritual growth. You may choose to provide copies of a reflection planner, such as *Servant Leader Journal for UMMen* (General Commission on United Methodist Men and United Methodist Communications, 1998). Another idea is to design a congregational booklet lifting up aspects of your local and connectional ministries to help members track their stewardship growth as part of their spiritual development. Or your congregation may offer a Money Autobiography Retreat, such as those led by the Ministry of Money and The Giving Project, in which participants reflect upon their money experiences in their families of origin and how those experiences now affect their life with money.

Words are important. We don't "take a collection"; we "give an offering." The way we receive the offering needs to fit our theology and current reality. Thomas Rieke, former United Methodist Associate General Secretary of the Section on Stewardship and current director of The Network for Charitable Giving, says passing the plate comes from old assumptions of weekly cash income and presents too passive an image for our response to God. So what can we do differently? We can provide a token or symbol for those who give in non-weekly ways. Givers can bring their financial and in-kind offerings to the Communion rail or to giving stations in the aisles. The offering can become a celebration of giving in a range of ways that show commitment and creativity.[2]

Before receiving the offering, the worship leader can tell stories of local or global ministries with a "Celebrating Our Connection" statement. A sentence written beneath the offering line in the bulletin followed by, "Now that's great stewardship!" can help people think about a Bible verse, a connectional ministry, or a quiet service done in or through the congregation.

Whatever form the offering takes, a prayer of dedication brings it all together before God. Mark Vincent's *Teaching a Christian View of Money: Celebrating God's Generosity* contains several pages of offertory prayers that may spark your own prayers of dedication.[3]

Creating a Climate for Generous Giving

Generosity is a sign of mental health. Reflecting on this connection, Bishop Kenneth Carder says that "giving is part of salvation. It is a means to and sign of emotional and spiritual health."[4]

Good health begins with diagnosis. Funding experts sometimes recommend using measurable indicators to assess our congregation's financial health. Why do we need objective tools to analyze where we are? Because otherwise we may cut spending at our ministry core; lay guilt on members for not giving enough; pick up programs and methods with conflicting theology; look for a "quick fix" to constant financial crises, ignoring underlying causes; or fail to assess how and why the congregation is doing what it's doing, including how it raises, manages, and spends funds for ministry.[5]

A three-year local-church stewardship plan helps in a number of ways. It allows us to design stewardship education as part of ongoing congregational life. It permits us to plan for changes within the natural rhythm of the church. It encourages us to emphasize different aspects of stewardship in different years. It helps us gain a positive outlook and create a healthy environment for stewardship development.

When a local church builds a climate for generous giving, the following elements often are at work:

• **Leader example**—The congregation's leaders not only "talk the talk" but also "walk the walk" in stewardship. They also know stewardship's Christian basis, how to cultivate giving (not the same as how to control finances), relationship skills, and the importance of communications. They are enthusiastic about the church and about their own involvement. They give their time and abilities, as well as a percentage of their finances, through the church. They support others who are trying to grow and present clear targets for commitment growth.

• **Proportionate giving, tithing, and beyond**—
Pastors and leaders use seasons of the Christian year and
ongoing ministries to teach and demonstrate proportionate giving, tithing, and going beyond the tithe.
They encourage not only individuals but the congregation as a whole to make gifts to the community, to
denominational ministries, and to ecumenical ministries.

• **Commitment Circle**—A healthy church
knows that people participate in the church on their
own terms, not on the church's terms. They participate
in the context of their total life involvements and how
well the congregation helps them meet their personal
goals. There are four patterns of church participation,
called the Commitment Circle, that arise from such
participation.[6]

1. About 5 percent of the members are "Creatives."
   They give generously of their time, energy, abilities,
   and money and bring considerable creativity to the
   church.

2. Another 15 to 20 percent are "Responsibles." They
   are very active, provide most of the leaders and volunteers, and are generous supporters. Together, the
   Creatives and Responsibles give about 75 percent of
   the church's donated income and 100 percent of its
   leadership.

3. Roughly 20 to 30 percent of the members are
   "Responsives." They identify with the church but
   attend infrequently. They respond to initiatives by

church leaders and attend all-church events if con-
tacted personally. They provide no leadership and
give about 25 percent of the congregation's income.

4. The other 45 to 60 percent of the members are "Dormants." They look to the church for baptisms, wed-
   dings, and funerals and for chaplaincy during turning
   points or crises. They may be former leaders who had
   a falling-out or who burnt out, may be family members of Creatives and Responsibles, and may attend
   at Christmas and Easter. They do not contribute
   time, leadership, or money.

This Commitment Circle is good news! With this
circle we can tailor contacts with people according to
their agenda, not ours. While Creatives and Responsibles get excited about the congregation's new ministries, Responsives respond to services that meet their
personal needs or the needs of their family at this stage.
Those whom God calls to visit Dormants commit
themselves to long-term, one-on-one relationships.

This means we don't need to dispirit enthusiastic
Creatives by sending them to visit Dormants with long-
standing complaints. We don't need to complain about
why some people do not come to the all-church planning retreat, or why some people do not pledge. We can
work to increase the committed percentages around the
circle. We can quit feeling bad about ourselves or others and resource people where they are.*

• **Giving patterns**—People have different giving
patterns. Many people receive regular paychecks and/or

Social Security checks. Pledgers often make their commitment to the church from their first check of the month. But a host of others—self-employed people such as farmers, sales people, freelance artists and writers, real-estate agents, and stockbrokers—do not have a regular income. They need church leaders to help them find ways to participate symbolically in the offering every week.

In addition, some congregations are able to take advantage of giving by electronic fund transfer (EFT). With this method, the bank automatically transfers the giver's amount each month into the church's account. For these givers, it is important to have a symbol to put into each Sunday's offering.

One way to include all non-weekly givers is to provide paper hearts in each week's bulletin that worshipers can give at the time of the offering. Before the offering, the worship leader can invite everyone to "give our hearts to God." This act can have great personal meaning for visitors and members alike.

Giving also fluctuates by season. After a summer slump, many churches receive December offerings that are three times larger than any other month of the year. Most church finance committees can anticipate cash flow by tracking giving by the month for the past five years. Reporting income by comparing Januaries, for example, gives a more realistic picture to the congregation. At year end, leaders can praise people for their generosity in past Decembers, tell them about people helped through their giving, and let them know what's needed to continue the congregation's excellent ministries.

Some cultures have strong stewardship traditions without pledging. For example, members of the Free Wesleyan Church of Tonga give through the *misinale*. Families or church classes save up for this lively annual event. When the day arrives, dancers or singers coat their skin with oil then celebrate both culture and spirituality. As these individuals share their talents, givers show appreciation by pressing dollar bills on them. It is a spiritual festival, as all give their best to God.

• **Planned giving**—Planned gifts are different from outright gifts in that they are meant to be fully realized in the future. Planned giving is giving beyond our lifetimes. It allows us to make greater gifts than we could from our current incomes, and it increases the church's financial resources. These gifts come from capital resources rather than from cash; they involve estate planning; they often give donors larger tax benefits than outright gifts and increased income from investments; and they're usually considerably larger than annual contributions.

So why don't church leaders talk much about planned giving? Most of us don't understand the technical side of tools such as wills, trusts, annuities, securities, real estate, retirement plans, bonds, pooled-income funds, and insurance policies. But jurisdictional and denominational agencies have experts, such as annual conference United Methodist Foundations and the stewardship experts at the General Board of Discipleship, who are willing to explain financial options.

Helping people with planned giving is a service to our members, regardless of whom they choose as beneficiaries. While members' incomes may have risen by only a few percentage points over recent years, in many regions the value of their land and property has increased. Many people are unaware of how to use these assets to support their Christian values and priorities.

Excellent resources are available to help us develop a planned-giving program in the local church. With these resources, we can help people learn about planned giving as a vital part of personal stewardship. We can encourage and acknowledge planned gifts, promote periodic will clinics or estate-planning workshops, and help our congregations develop committees to encourage bequests and provide guidelines to support future ministries.

Preaching the Richness of Stewardship

Stewardship is "the economics of conversion," says Patricia Wilson-Kastner.[7] It is living out what happens when we center our lives in God. So stewardship includes not only how to care for all the things and relationships of this life, but also why we care for them: what we are trying to do in the world on God's behalf. Stewardship is overseeing every resource of life for God!

Everything we do has a stewardship dimension, and every Sunday's Bible text embraces it. We can preach stewardship throughout the year in its trinitarian richness. Here are some possibilities.

Gifts of Creation

Time

Exodus 20:8-11	Sabbath and Shalom: Rest, Work, and Wholeness
Ecclesiastes 3:1-8	Time as Burden or Gift? Matthew 24:36-44 Now's the Time! (*kairos*)
Luke 9:57-62	No More Business-As-Usual
Luke 14:25-30	Planning Ahead (chronos)
Ephesians 5:15-20	First Things First: Living God's Priorities
Colossians 4:2-6	Too Busy Not to Pray
2 Peter 3:8-14	Living Between Two Advents (aion)

Talents

John 9:1-15	Spreading God's Sight
1 Corinthians 6:19-20	Put Your Body Into It
Matthew 5:3-16	Using What You've Got
Matthew 22:34-40	God's Magnificent Reversal (love God through neighbor)

Money and Possessions

Deuteronomy 26:1-15	Tithing for Justice
Exodus 36	More Than Enough
2 Chronicles 31:4-10	Firstfruits Giving
Matthew 19:16-30	When Things Get in the Way
Luke 10:29-37	Going All Out for a Stranger
Luke 12:13-21	When Our Riches Rob Us
Luke 14:31-33	Giving It All Away
Luke 16:1-13	Money and Power: Using Them Well
Luke 16:19-31	Rich and Poor: Bridging the Gulf
Luke 19:1-10	Gratitude Attitude
Luke 21:1-4	When a Little Is More Than a Lot
Acts 2:42-47	Economics for Life
Acts 5:1-11	When We Try to Cheat God
Acts 6:1-6	Sharing What We Have
2 Corinthians 8:1-15	Overflowing Generosity: A Matter of Balance
2 Corinthians 9:6-8	God's Abundance: You Can't Give It Away!

The Earth

Gifts of Redemption

The Gospel

1 Corinthians 12:1-13	Use It or Lose It: Spiritual Gifts for the Church
Ephesians 4:11-16	Body Building (for the Body of Christ)

Ministry of the Church

Matthew 25:31-46	Doing Our Least for the Least? Matthew 28:16-20 Don't Just Do Something
Luke 8:19-21	Walkin' the Talk
Acts 1:1-8	The Pinwheel Effect (of witnessing)
Romans 9:20-26	The Angry Pot: Agreeing to God's Plan
Romans 12:3-5	Follow Your Gift: Passion and Perspective
1 Corinthians 3:21-4:2	Stewards of God's Mysteries
2 Corinthians 6:3-13	Widening Our Hearts
Hebrews 13:12-13	Going Outside the Camp
1 Peter 2:4-10	Living Stones, or Plain Old Rocks?

Brian Bauknight recommends these ten guidelines for developing great stewardship preaching:

1. Be bold. Jesus spoke more about money and possessions than any other subject except the reign of God, so we never need to apologize for speaking about it as part of Christian life.
2. Be upbeat.

3. Put giving in the context of discipleship.
4. Talk about your own experience: how you learned to give, signposts along the way, and the next step for you in your giving journey.
5. Model good growth-giving.
6. Preach, teach, and practice tithing.
7. Teach and preach the gift of giving.
8. Be creative with sermon titles, texts, and themes.
9. Use humor, including plays on words. For example: "A Farewell to Alms" says giving isn't a matter of dues or donations but of substantive response to God's mercies as an adventurous act of discipleship. "Put a Tither in Your Tank" urges people to give God's ministry real get-up-and-go!
10. Work for the long haul, cultivating new givers, new "conversions" to a stewarding life, one step at a time.[8]

Experiencing Freedom in Proportionate Giving

While the tithe, or ten percent, is often considered the norm for Christian giving, members of most mainline churches fall far short of that percentage. Many of us have not learned to think of our giving by percentages, as opposed to a flat amount. But proportionate giving—giving a percentage of our income, whatever it may be—encourages Christians to decide upfront what they will offer back to God through the church. Proportionate giving emphasizes intentional giving, regardless of the amount of our financial resources. It also gives us the freedom to start wherever we are and keep growing. We may stretch from one percent to two percent, from two to five, from ten to twenty or more, depending upon our life circumstances and living out of gratitude to God.

When church leaders practice proportionate (percentage) giving, they spark at least six great things: (1) greater dreams for the congregation as a result of trust in leadership; (2) more risk-taking within the church family; (3) focus upon the future, not upon maintaining the status quo; (4) a challenge for others to join them in intentional giving; (5) an atmosphere of freedom to share about money and spiritual issues; and (6) discovery that giving our money leads to giving ourselves.

Ten percent is not a magic number. In fact, the Bible speaks about multiple tithes and offerings. In Deuteronomy 26, for example, God tells the people to give the first of their crops as well as tithes and offerings in yearly cycles. Their giving is to be an act of worship out of thanksgiving to God. It links giving with celebration, supports those without economic means, and empowers religious workers to give a lifetime of service.

Tithing is a means, not an end. Jesus uses humor to criticize those who become legalistic about tithing (even giving ten percent of their cooking spices), while they neglect the "weightier matters" of "justice and mercy and faith" (Matthew 23:23-24). At the same time, he affirms both tithing and financial generosity, regardless of the amount given (Luke 21:1-4).

One way we can return to the concept of giving our whole selves is to focus on what has been called firstfruits living. Through firstfruits living we give the first and the best of our lives to God as an act of worship. Then we find ways to honor God as we use the rest of the resources God has given us to manage.

How refreshing! Firstfruits living lifts up all of our resources and relationships, not just the religious ones. It prompts us to retell God's faithful acts; to offer ourselves back to God in love; to host fellowship feasts and support buildings as houses of worship and service; and to use all of our roles (not only the role of church member) as points of distribution for those in need. Firstfruits living is a lifestyle, the dedication of one's whole life.

So the issue is not how much we have. It's not even how much we give. Rather, it's what we do with all that God has given us. Proportionate giving beckons us on a spiritual journey that invites us to grow.

Stewarding Year Round

Nationwide stewardship leader Thomas Rieke has designed a funding cycle that captures the natural flow of ministry planning, implementation, and resourcing throughout the local-church year. By looking at our congregational life in this way, we discover a framework for planning stewardship year round.

The Funding Cycle[9]

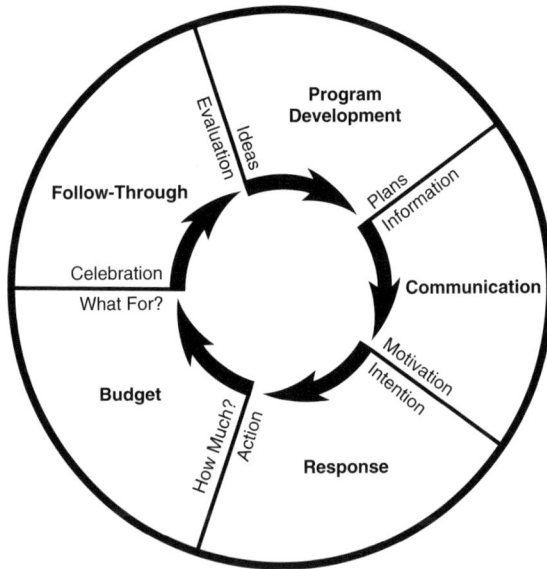

Each dimension leads into the next, building upon our work together and encouraging fuller participation.

Program Development—We look first, not at overwhelming needs to fill, but at who we are as God's people (our identity) and the particular vision God has given us (our ministry). We can begin to move from *ideas* to *plans* in various ways, including an in-person survey of the congregation, home meetings to share dreams for future ministries, a survey series during worship, and interviews of community leaders, followed by a church leaders' planning retreat.

A look at the program development area clarifies our congregation's identity and ministry and shows how these intersect with people's needs. When we share ideas widely within the church family, people identify with the process, discover others with similar dreams, develop enthusiasm, and anticipate church plans to come.

Communication—Communication moves people from *information* to *motivation* in ways that are personal, persuasive, and positive. Communication stresses listening to hear where people are and what they dream for the future. We share stories about people whose lives are being changed, thanks to generous gifts from the church.

Year-round person-to-person communication empowers faith and strengthens relationships. For example, San Francisco's Jones Memorial United Methodist Church, a vibrant African American inner-city congregation, has Home Life Ministries, groups of twelve to fifteen people who meet in homes for worship, Bible study, and conversation. All the groups use monthly worship booklets written by the church's multiple lay leaders to reinforce Christian growth and stewardship.

One exciting way to tell stories is to send monthly letters to the congregation from different people affected by the church's ministries. Writers may include a Sunday school child, a member of the youth group, someone involved in the outreach program, a new member, and so forth.[10]

Response—Once the congregation has generated ideas, transformed them into plans, and told stories about changing lives, members of the faith community have the chance to give, moving from *intention* to *action*. At this stage, people have the opportunity to respond with their money, time, talents, and abilities to support the congregation's plans for ministry. Notice that they are not pledging to the budget; the final budget hasn't been formulated yet. Rather, they are pledging to fund and participate in the ministries that will accomplish their goals.

A number of response programs are available for the every-member-commitment effort. Whatever form and style you use, make it simple and easy for people to respond. Also provide opportunities year round for those who want to update their commitments or who weren't on board during the stewardship effort. For example, have commitment cards available and interpret their use in new-member classes; provide a Lenten study of spiritual disciplines or classes on the Wesleyan heritage; or plan an experimental month of tithing, in which members are encouraged to commit to tithing for that month with no expectation or commitment beyond then.

Budget—After members have responded, church leaders can formulate the budget. The traditional line-item budget answers the question, How much? While necessary for internal committee accountability, a focus on how much is not a motivating tool. Once leaders have determined the basic figures, they can turn the line items into a narrative budget (in sentence form) and so help the congregation move from, *How much?* to, *What for?*

A narrative budget describes the ministries that your church plans for the coming year. For each dimension of service, such as community outreach, two paragraphs might describe the ministry. Then one sentence states, for example, "Twenty percent of our budget (approximately $28,000) enables us to spread the Christian faith in tangible ways in our community."

Such a budget has several benefits:

1. It presents ministry spending in relation to the local church's vision statement or by major dimensions of the congregation's work. The instrument may cluster activities by mission-statement sentences; by seasons of the Christian year; by dimensions of service (such as worship, outreach, Christian education, care for people); or by age-level or other significant ministries.

2. It encourages a perspective that sees salaries and facilities as channels for ministry instead of as overhead. The costs of personnel and property are divided into ministry dimensions according to percentages of time used for different purposes.

3. It helps members see church programs as building blocks that they can prioritize and support, whether through a unified budget or through extra-mile designated giving.

4. It focuses on what the church is planning, not on maintaining what already exists, thereby connecting people to unfolding mission.

5. It communicates more effectively than do line-item amounts, since it says what the church will do with money received.

6. It prompts people to think proportionately (by percentages) about the congregation's giving. Thinking proportionately helps them remember the context of their church's total ministry and strengthens proportionate giving as a personal spiritual discipline.

Follow-through—This stage begins by thanking all who were involved in the cycle of program development, communication, response, and budget design. It includes reporting the results: ministries planned, funding responses, and member participation. Quarterly stories (or better, monthly letters) highlight the difference the church makes in people's lives and strengthen each giver's sense of connection with the global church.

Good follow-through embraces most of the year as members move from *celebration* to *evaluation*. Follow-through prepares for further idea generation and planning as the Funding Cycle begins again.

When we plan stewardship year round, boredom never sets in. Each year, leaders emphasize a different section of the ministry cycle. Members come closer to one another as they dream and implement plans together, learn more about the church's ministry, and experience the congregation as a community of growing stewards.

Mobilizing People

Time is a gift, not a burden to be managed or crammed full with dubious activities. Joyful stewards can learn to put first things first and help others relearn the gift of time. Three New Testament words reflect different ways we are stewards of time. *Chronos* is the span from past to present to future, time measured in the order in which things happen. As good stewards, we plan ahead, taking one day at a time and making the most of the *chronos* given us. *Aion* refers to God's eternity, the everlasting time promised us beyond this lifetime. As stewards, we live in hope, oriented to life in fullness with God. *Kairos* is the unexpected crystalline moment that shimmers with special meaning. It is that God-given moment that is filled with possibilities. Like Moses' burning bush, *kairos* prompts us to wake up to God, stand in wonder, and respond to the unique opportunity.

Talents are the abilities that every human being has: body, mind, soul, and strength. The Old Testament concept of self had no division between body and soul. Jesus expressed this unity in the great commandment. He said, "You shall love the Lord your God with all your heart, and with all your soul, and with all your mind, and with all your strength" (Mark 12:30)—in other words, with all that you are.

Stephen Covey, Roger Merrill, and Rebecca Merrill say that the physical, mental, social, and spiritual dimensions of who we are can overlap and integrate. Once we recognize our talents in all of these areas and

are stewards of them, the result is a spontaneous com-
bustion of passion and vision.[11]

Individual spiritual gifts are the gifts of grace that
God gives to people for particular purposes in a congregation or ministry. Resources abound on how to discover our spiritual gifts. (Patricia Brown's *SpiritGifts* is
especially creative and user-friendly for a retreat or
class.)

In the Scriptures, we find lists of such gifts in
Romans 12:3-8; 1 Corinthians 12:4-11; 1 Corinthians
12:27-31; and Ephesians 4:7-16. They include (but are
not limited to) prophecy, pastoring, teaching, encour-
agement (exhortation), giving, compassion, wisdom,
knowledge, faith, healing, miracles, discernment,
tongues, interpretation, apostleship, assisting, leadership, and evangelism.

How we visualize using these gifts in the local
church makes a difference. For example, if we assume
the usual top-down accountability chart as our model,
we imply a hierarchy of gifts as well as of power. A more
corporate model comes from the Center for Parish
Development. It pictures the congregation as overlapping circles of formal and informal teams. The circles
connect through "linking" people, who belong to both
groups, sharing ideas and energy in both directions.[12]

How can we use these individual gifts in the congregation as part of a system to create and implement
ministries? *NetWork* is one resource that describes a
process of organizing the congregation's ministries
through the lens of individual spiritual gifts. The

approach includes teaching and implementation by pastoral leadership, members' exploration of their gifts, training and choice of service area from among options, and follow-up with the giver on his or her ministry.[13]

Christ United Methodist Church, a three-thousand-member church in Bethel Park, Pennsylvania, began using *NetWork* in 1996. After three years, they had more than three hundred graduates, all serving in or through the local church. Cindy Olszewski, program director, finds *NetWork* unique among spiritual-gifts resources in its identification of three factors: one's passion (area of ministry), one's spiritual gifts, and one's working style.

Christ Church offers spiritual gifts classes throughout the year. After participants take the class and gifts inventories, they have an individual interview. At that time, a Gifts Mentor helps them choose three possible places to serve in one of three hundred ministry options. Children and youth go through the process as well. No amount of time is too little to offer for service.

Crystal Springs United Methodist Church, a one-hundred-member congregation in San Mateo, California, created their own way to organize and use individual spiritual gifts. Calling stewardship "discipleship in action," they have a Coordinator of Volunteer Ministries who helps constituents discover their gifts through a survey, a time-and-talent inventory, and a personal interview. Then they train the constituents in their new roles. The coordinator helps leaders form ministry descriptions, shape and consecrate ministry teams, and recognize those involved in these one-year ministry team commitments.

Focusing on Each Generation

If stewardship is whatever we do with the good news by the way we live, then it affects our relationships, priorities, and passions; our planning and values; and our use of time, abilities, money, and assets. But we don't automatically know how to recognize and use our abilities in the church and community, how to manage our money, how to give first to God, or how to live on our income. So we need to start learning stewardship from childhood.

Children and youth can become generous, joyful stewards! A key ingredient is recognizing teachable moments for stewardship in their lives. They learn positive stewardship messages when they participate in and learn from structured experiences, such as participating in worship, visiting a sick or lonely friend, exercising, praying, talking about Jesus, planting a garden, practicing good nutrition, and developing positive relationships. Children resonate to stories, learning ways to relate Bible stories to their daily lives.

Youth jump into a variety of stewardship activities, including writing skits, taking a ministry tour of the church building, giving gifts to missionaries, designing a stewardship board game, meeting outreach-project leaders, planning stewardship-themed puppet shows, tithing their allowance, and participating in congregational decisions.

Adults' perspectives vary by age.[14] Members of the *GI Generation* (also called *Builders*) were born between 1910 and 1927. GIs are strongly civic-oriented. They tend to believe that history moves in orderly, straight lines. They're concerned that virtue is being lost among the younger generations. Members of the *Pioneer Generation* (also known as the *Silent Generation*) were born between 1928 and 1945. Pioneers tend to be other-directed, and they highly esteem process and expertise. They also tend toward nonjudgmental fairness and open-mindedness. Both the Pioneer and GI Generations are well-represented in most North American congregations.

Baby Boomers are the one-in-three Americans who were born between 1946 and 1963. The Baby Boomers sway North American society with their values and trends. Most of them acknowledge the "visionary" personality of their generation, which tends to focus on principles or moral issues.

Boomers hold four values in common with other generations—home, marriage, family, and work—but they shape them differently from other age groups. Home for Baby Boomers is a place of refuge but also a time-pressured environment where two incomes are required to pay for housing. Men and women share responsibilities, family members function independently, and children have their own opinions. Two-thirds of Baby Boomers consider weekends family time. Three out of five Baby Boomers see their work as a career, but they don't want to wait too long to achieve their goals. They focus on self-fulfillment (in contrast to the self-sacrifice of the GI Generation), instant gratification, emotional expressiveness, and hands-on ministry.[15]

Members of the *Postmodern Generation* (also known as Gen Xers, Busters, or Thirteeners) were born between 1964 and 1981. Although a smaller group than the Baby Boomers, they include sixty-eight million people.[16] Skeptical about sociological groupings, they are proud survivors. They grew up fast and experienced childhood during rising divorce and poverty rates, in a time of experimental classrooms and latchkey kids. They became young singles in the post-AIDS social scene.

Taken together, these two generations born since World War II (the Baby Boomers and the Postmoderns) embody "the electronic culture." Having grown up with television, they find computers reshaping their perspectives daily. The church must communicate stewardship to them in electronic language, offering images and music to convey the message.[17]

Congregations wanting to work with the electronic culture need to

1. open the church doors to those who have had religious experiences outside the church and to unmarried adults living with partners (who have more than 700,000 children among them).

2. provide handles for basic understandings of faith and avenues for service. Focus on the Bible, the

church's beginnings, and how God can help people get through the week.

3. offer stability and a sense of connectedness. Boomers move an average of once every three years, and their family members live far away.

4. explore changes in program and schedule. One congregation takes members by bus to a weekly hands-on service project. Another local church regularly caters a meal, with childcare, for young adults from their church and other denominations in the area.

5. find ways to work with short-term commitments. One church has no annual funding effort but provides a fund drive every six weeks. Another has a quarterly Tithe Sunday.

6. offer a "high-quality package" that gives options; positive folk theology; and user-friendly, community-oriented programs in well-kept facilities for children and young adults.[18]

Underneath these recommendations is a different paradigm (way of perceiving and acting) of the church. Thomas Bandy describes the shift in *Kicking Habits: Welcome Relief for Addicted Churches*, when he contrasts the English game of croquet with the Central American game of *jai alai* (pronounced high lie).[19] He says that the old way of doing things at church is like croquet. Movement is managed, controlled, subtle, and self-contained. All moves must pass through the central wicket of meetings every time. Players move one by one, go through the hoops, and can be sent to the edges of the field by power players.

Not so with thriving churches that include younger-adult generations. *Jai alai* is a fast-paced game where players use curved wicker rackets to catch, redirect, and hurl a ball. In *jai alai*-style churches, participants, like balls, are already speeding on a spiritual journey, propelled by their hunger for a Higher Power. Church leaders accelerate the balls by centrifugal force, so members are changed, gifted, called, equipped, and sent out in a new direction. Instead of settling into a croquet home in the church, they fire back out into society, *jai-alai* fashion.

Funding for Ministry

Follow the Cycle Theory. Donald Joiner, operations officer and director of fund development for Discipleship Ministries at the General Board of Discipleship of The United Methodist Church, has developed a Cycle Theory to help us use a variety of well-grounded programs to invite members to fund the church's ministry.[20]

Cycle Theory

Year One:
Celebration
Sunday

YearThree:
Quick and Easy

Year Two:
One-on-One Communication

A congregation may use the same type of effort for one or two years then move to the next. All three types first subtract the Dormants (who are visited individually outside the funding context) and send a mailing to introduce the approach. Within each response type, there are a number of published funding programs available.

1. The *Celebration Sunday* model focuses on one Sunday when church family members celebrate the ministry of their church and then make their commitments. The worship service may be followed by a catered meal. It is essential, however, to recognize that only one-third to one-half of the church members will be present on any one Sunday to participate in this program. You will need to plan to tell the stories in other ways as well.

2. *One-on-One Communication* approaches provide personal interaction using a variety of methods. Some members may receive information in small group meetings, possibly meeting in the homes of members. Others may receive a personal phone call or visit. Some congregations may plan an open house where members can visit booths that illustrate the church's ministries and provide opportunities to pledge time as well as money.

3. *Quick and Easy* response efforts attempt to involve as many people as possible with little personal contact and minimal committee effort. They include passing packets from house to house and using direct mail to the total membership.

Talk about money. Many pastors and church leaders have been afraid to talk about money for fear of being judged as institution-oriented or self-serving. But people want to know how to handle money so that it doesn't control them, how to use money wisely and well for God in all areas of life, and how to give money for God's uses through the church.

Giving is an essential part of authentic discipleship. Financial giving is giving our whole selves to God and seeking first God's reign.[21] Pastors must boldly state the need for faithful financial stewardship, knowing that it stands on strong Christian and Wesleyan traditions, and that it begins and ends in praising God.[22]

People are drawn to clear connections between ministry and money. For example, one fourteen-hundred-member congregation in Florida isn't afraid to talk about money or personal-involvement ministries that attract seekers of all ages. In late 1995 the church moved into a forty-thousand-square-foot building on twenty-one acres of land. This move meant voting for a mortgage of 2.5 million dollars—and members applauded the decision. How did this act of faith happen? The church's pastor regularly talked about money related to spiritual development, particularly in Lent. In new-member classes, he encouraged participants to try proportionate giving as part of Christian growth.

Interpret mission giving constantly, even in the smallest congregation. Church leaders help when they openly ask the question, Where does our money go? then share personal stories culled from denominational resources such as *Sharing God's Gifts* and the annual *United Methodist Prayer Calendar*.

It's like planting seeds. For the good news to sink in, we need to keep hearing stories through multiple channels. Stories can come to us as sermon illustrations, in the newsletter, in the bulletin, from special worship speakers, and in congregational mission- and community-building events. Paired with hands-on experiences such as Volunteers In Mission, Sierra Service Project, and more, these stories help spin the congregation into meaningful, vibrant ministries.

Great giving churches come in all sizes. Ogden Friendship House United Methodist Church is a congregation of twenty-one members in a small town in Kansas. Each Sunday they place dots on wall maps as they pray for ministries listed in the United Methodist

Prayer Calendar. They give to the denomination's special offerings and talk about where the money goes. Each week in worship they give a hunger offering by passing around a plastic two-liter bottle for Heifer Project, buying more animals each year. They pay their denominational benevolences in full, invite missionaries to speak, and have a covenant relationship with a missionary in Nepal.

Provide top-quality fund management, another key ingredient in funding for ministry. Such management assures members that accountable church leaders use their local dollars responsibly. Fund management does not have to be a complex process, but it needs to be a consistent one.

Connect the giver and the receiver. Local leaders need to connect givers with receivers in several ways throughout the year. For example, when making financial reports to the congregation, tell the congregation what the giving has done (how many children are learning from the curriculum, and so forth). Plan to send new members on an outreach project soon after their confirmation. Write thank-you letters for in-kind donations and gifts of time. Hold ethnic festivals for countries where missionaries whom you support live. Write to missionaries on their birthdays.

In Olathe, Kansas, Grace United Methodist Church emphasizes congregational mission trips and Volunteers in Mission (VIM). The congregation sends out one adult medical team and two youth teams annually. The adult team works in the same medical clinic in Mexico every year. Sparked by a youth VIM team that went there in 1986, Grace United Methodist Church has helped the local residents build a clinic, a dormitory, and a church. In a joint effort with Dayspring United Methodist Church in Tempe, Arizona, they provide salary support year round for the clinic's doctor.

When members of Olathe Grace planned to move to a new location in 1999, they intended to sell their facilities, which had a replacement value of 4.5 million dollars. But when the property didn't sell, the congregation moved anyway and turned the old campus into a mission center. Expanding their focus in the local community, they continued their programs for youth, senior ministries, daycare, English as a Second Language classes, clothes closet, and food pantry in the largely blue-collar and Hispanic community, and leased the gym to community groups.

Making the Journey Our Home

By now it's clear that stewardship is not an endpoint we achieve but a lifetime process of spiritual growth. As with Jewish mitzvot and John Wesley's means of grace, our actions on God's behalf give us signposts along our stewardship path with God.

Like Moses' people in the wilderness, we travel on our stewardship journey as God's people, not having arrived at our final destination of total faithfulness, but always on the way. We take steps along the journey, and the journey is our home.

A Smoldering Wilderness

For a long time now, we have lived with the myth of
scarcity. Walter Brueggemann, Old Testament scholar,
says that consumerism confronts North American
Christians as a central problem of our lives. It presents
the conflict between our attraction to the good news of
God's abundance on the one hand, and the power of
our belief in scarcity on the other hand. Scarcity works
on fear that God's grace will run out. It assumes that
money is security and that there won't be enough
resources for all. Based on market economics, scarcity
begins not with our limited needs but with our unlim-
ited wants. As long as we believe that more is always
better, we will never have enough.

Yet the Bible is a sweeping witness to God's generosity and life-giving power. It begins in Genesis 1
with a song praising God's generosity. The manna of
Exodus 16 echoes in 2 Corinthians 8:9: "For your sakes
he [Jesus] became poor, so that by his poverty you might
become rich." Embodying Mary's song, Jesus revealed
the reign of God as a different kind of economy, one
that is infused with abundance and self-giving generosity. Living out our gratitude, we are called to trust God's
generosity.[23]

God's overflowing gifts pour out of God's action in
the world—God's creating, redeeming, and empowering love. They flow out of God's trinitarian activity
with human beings and within creation. Such abundance invites us to a lifestyle of planned simplicity,
advocacy, celebration, and sharing.[24]

We began this journey with Moses' meeting God in a burning bush. For all we know, God might have set thousands of bushes on fire all across Midian during previous months, hoping to catch Moses' attention. I can imagine an aerial view of Midian as a smoldering wilderness, with Moses wandering through day after day, asking, "Where is God, anyway? If I could just have a sign!"

We live in a smoldering wilderness filled with burning bushes! In the midst of abundance, God waits eagerly for us. Will we notice this bush, or that one? God lights them all, hoping we'll notice one. Will we trust God's abundance when our society insists upon scarcity thinking and behavior? Will we continue to believe the myth of scarcity? Or will we use the wealth of resources God has already given us?

As you and I wander through such a wilderness, each in our own place of ministry, God wants to turn us around so that God can give us an entirely different identity and ministry from what we may have assumed before. As the poet says, "every common bush" may be "afire with God,"[25] waiting for us to notice and to turn aside.

Spirited stewardship can teach us to become communities of stewards setting the world afire with the gospel of Jesus Christ! We need only follow the Spirit, then fan the flames.

Questions and Activities

All congregations want to reach people with meaningful ministry. While we can continue some things that
are positive and effective, we need to change other
approaches to be more focused and fruitful. We may
even need to shift our whole paradigm for what we are
about and how we will live out the stewardship of the
gospel in our new setting.

- What things that are already part of your local
  church can you build upon to express fully the depth
  of stewardship? What images, understandings, or
  practices of stewardship can you begin to change?
- How can you focus your own biblically-based vision
  of stewardship in your personal spiritual journey and
  put it into practice?
- What insights from this book do you want to explore
  with your congregation so that they can become a
  more joyous and faithful community of stewards?

For Reflection

- In *Hymns From the Four Winds: A Collection of Asian
  American Hymns* (Abingdon Press, 1983), Hymn No.
  112 pairs a prayer for God's "powerful hand" with a
  pledge to "give a helping hand" to free the earth from
  hate, greed, and prejudice. In what ways can you
  work together with others within the church, community, and nation to change systems that assume
  ownership and domination instead of
  stewardship/koinonia for God?

- Read the words to "What Gift Can We Bring" (*The United Methodist Hymnal*, 87). Write down phrases that speak to you. What steps can you take to deepen your stewardship of the gospel?

Endnotes

1 See *Teaching a Christian View of Money: Celebrating God's Generosity*, by Mark Vincent (Herald Press, 1997); page 32.

2 See "The Passing of the Passing of the Plates," by Thomas C. Rieke, in *The Clergy Journal*, February 1999.

3 See *Teaching a Christian View of Money: Celebrating God's Generosity*, by Mark Vincent (Herald Press, 1997); pages 40–44.

4 From "Reflections: Giving as a Sign of Emotional Health," by Bishop Kenneth Carder, in *Memphis Conference United Methodist Reporter*, November 6, 1998. Used by permission.

5 See *Get Well! Stay Well! Prescriptions for a Financially Healthy Congregation*, by Wayne C. Barrett (Discipleship Resources, 1997). See pages 13–17 for examples of diagnostic tools.

6 See *Designs in Fund Raising*, by Harold Seymour (McGraw Hill, 1950), and Every-Member Visits in Your Church, by Paul M. Dietterich (The Center for Parish Development, 1986).

7 See "Preaching Stewardship: An Every-Sunday Theme," by Patricia Wilson-Kastner, from the *Stewardship Resources for Mission and Ministry* series (Ecumenical Center for Stewardship Studies, 1993); page 2.

8 Adapted from "A New Generosity: Discipled Giving for the Local Church," a seminar by Brian Bauknight,

June 28, 1999, in Oakland, California. Used by permission.

9   By Thomas C. Rieke, The Network for Charitable Giving, 7700 Edgewater Dr., Suite 847, Oakland, CA 94621; phone 510-569-5580. Used by permission.

10 See *Letters for All Seasons: Telling the Church's Story by Mail*, by Herbert Mather (Section on Stewardship, General Board of Discipleship).

11 See *First Things First: To Live, to Love, to Learn, to Leave a Legacy*, by Stephen R. Covey, A. Roger Merrill, and Rebecca R. Merrill (Fireside, Simon & Schuster, 1994); pages 48–49.

12 See *Leadership Skills for Church Vitalization: Resource Book* (Center for Parish Development, 1976).

13 *NetWork: The Right People, In the Right Places, For the Right Reasons*, by Bruce Bugbee, Don Cousins, and Bill Hybels (Zondervan, 1994); includes a Participant's Guide, Implementation Guide, Leader's Guide, and training videotape.

14 See *Generations: The History of America's Future, 1584-2069*, by William Strauss and Neil Howe (Quill, 1991), and Dynamics of Generational Stewardship, by Bradley G. Call (sponsored by The Stewardship Committee of the East Ohio Conference of The United Methodist Church, 1996).

15 See *Reaching for the Baby Boomers* (General Board of Discipleship, 1989); video and workbook.

16 In the year 2000, per the United States Bureau of the Census.

17 See *The Spectacle of Worship in a Wired World: Electronic Culture and the Gathered People of God*, by Tex Sample (Abingdon Press, 1998).

18 See "Our Missing Generation and Six Strategies *for Reaching Boomers," by Warren Hartman, in Reaching for*